REAL MURDER INVESTIGATIONS

An Insider's View

Kevin Moore

Published by Saron Publishers in 2019

Copyright © Kevin Moore 2019
All rights reserved

No part of this publication may be reproduced, stored in a retrieval system, or transmitted, in any form or by any means, without the prior permission in writing of the publisher, nor be otherwise circulated in any form of binding or cover other than that in which it is published and without a similar condition including this condition being imposed on the subsequent purchaser

Copyright © All photos Kevin Moore

ISBN-13: 978-1-913297-00-8

Saron Publishers
Pwllmeyrick House
Mamhilad
Mon
NP4 8RG

www.saronpublishers.co.uk

info@saronpublishers.co.uk

Follow us on Facebook and Twitter

THE HOMICIDE INVESTIGATOR'S CREED

No greater honour will ever be bestowed on an officer, or a more profound duty imposed on him, than when he is entrusted with the investigation of the death of another human being.

DEDICATION

This book is dedicated to two very important people in my life.

Firstly, my wife Ann, whose support and encouragement over the years helped me to achieve all that I have.

Secondly, my father, former Police Sergeant John Moore, who, despite his premature death, has been my inspiration throughout my police career.

Finally, it is dedicated to all those fine police officers, both past and present, who have been involved in the investigation of murder. Every one of you is a member of a great club!

AUTHOR'S CHARITY

All profits from the sale of the book are going to the police related charity COPS – Care of Police Survivors.

ACKNOWLEDGEMENTS

I wish to begin by thanking my publisher, Penny Reeves of the Saron Publishers, for her time, patience, sound professional advice and understanding once again in helping me to write and then publish this book.

Whilst this book is about murder investigation and includes my involvement in many of the cases referred to, I wish to pay tribute to those officers and staff who worked with or for me during all of those occasions. Murder investigation is very much a team effort and what I have written is, I hope, a testimony to the many individuals who have previously worked and continue to work in what is the most challenging of policing environments. Their expertise and professionalism will always remain in my memory.

Also, I wish to thank my many friends and colleagues for their unwavering support and friendship over the period of my long career. There are simply too many to list the names of here. However, you will all know who you are. Without you, what I have achieved over the years would not have been possible. Policing, perhaps more than any other profession in existence, relies on the men and women who serve within it for their dedication, team work, courage and public spiritedness. It has been my privilege to have worked with some of the very best in this regard.

I have had the privilege of working for some of the very best Senior Investigating Officers (SIOs) in my early years of involvement on murder investigations. I have learned so much from them and it is without doubt largely down to them that I was able to achieve what I did as an investigator.

As the Homicide Investigators Creed has laid down, it was truly an honour for me to have been entrusted with the investigation of the deaths of others. I always aspired to do the very best that I could on behalf of them and their families. I hope that those who follow on behind me and the others like me always feel the same.

FOREWORD

Murder is brutal and the most violent of crimes. However, despite this, the majority of the population are fascinated with murder and its investigation. This has led to a huge growth over the years, not only in media coverage but also in its dramatisation in TV fiction, as well as the showing of true crime stories.

So why is this? Does the human race possess an inbuilt morbid curiosity about murder and its portrayal? Is the population somehow perverted in attempting to assuage its apparent thirst for such coverage? High viewing numbers are guaranteed for any television programme containing police-related stories. There seems to be a certain romance, whether in fiction or in documentaries, regarding police investigation into instances of major crime and in particular those involving murder.

Kevin Moore, the author of this book, is a retired senior police officer who spent the vast majority of his police career as a detective and ended his police service as Head of the CID (Criminal Investigation Department) in Sussex Police. During his time, he was involved at all levels and ranks in many murder investigations. Therefore, he has considerable knowledge and experience of what is involved in investigating these most violent of crimes.

In this book, he explores the seemingly endless public obsession with the act of murder itself. The book then moves on to consider the reality of such investigations, as opposed to the fictional portrayal. Kevin discusses the ways in which murder investigation over the years has fundamentally changed and how this is reflected in the resources now used. He also deals with the ways in which the professionalisation of such enquiries has developed. He is quick to point out, however, that much of the learning comes from those who have been involved in such investigations previously. Indeed, he acknowledges that much of his own learning came from those with whom he worked over the years.

Throughout the book, in order to highlight the elements involved in murder investigation, Kevin uses case studies taken from enquiries in which he was involved or which he led. Most of these are, therefore, related to Sussex. However, he has also included other cases which highlight particular issues that he feels help the reader to understand.

This therefore makes for a very interesting account of the developments in murder investigation over the years. It helps the reader understand the thought processes used by those leading such cases.

The final part of the book considers how murder investigation may develop further in the future, as policing faces funding pressures identical to other public sector organisations. This will need careful handling as the folly of 'cutting corners' in such cases has considerable consequences.

The book is also a tribute to all those police officers who have been involved in such cases. These events are rightly high-profile and so there is considerable exposure and pressure for those involved. Decision-making is therefore tested, not only through judicial proceedings but often through the media also. There is massive public interest in murder and its investigation. Involvement in such cases is not for everyone and is certainly not for the faint-hearted!

However, most of those who have undertaken the role of homicide investigators over the years recognize the huge privilege involved in investigating the deaths of fellow human beings. This is a key element of the homicide investigator's creed as included at the start of the book.

CONTENTS

1	The Dramatisation of and the Morbid Fascination With Murder	13
2	Legal Definitions and Defences in Law	24
3.	Professionalisation of Murder Investigation Over the Years	38
4	The Reality – The Set Up For a Murder Investigation	49
5	The Role of the Senior Investigating Officer	65
6	So, Is It a Murder?	88
7	Victims and Their Families	104
8	Murder Reviews	126
9	Unresolved or 'Cold'/Unsolved Cases	143
10	The Future of Murder Investigation	163

CHAPTER 1
The Dramatisation of and The Morbid Fascination With Murder

It was shortly after 10pm on Monday 23rd October 1978 when young PC AM758 Kevin Moore, a relatively recent recruit to the Sussex Police, took up his duty of guarding the deposition site for the body of murder victim, Margaret Frame. This was my very first involvement in a murder investigation, albeit a relatively minor one. Although I did not appreciate it at the time, it was to lead to my being involved in many such investigations as both a junior, and later a senior, investigator. I spent the whole night shift alone, accompanied only by my flask and sandwiches, looking after this site in a wooded area of Stanmer Park, Brighton. It was distinctly lonely and dark, and a very long time without a single soul to see or speak to. Nowadays, I dare say a huge fuss would be made if an individual were directed to undertake similar duties! Later on, I will discuss this case, which remains unsolved to this day.

I use the case, and my minor involvement, to highlight the fact that murder investigation is, and always has been, far more complex and resource-intensive than many fictional depictions would have us believe! When we see fictional detectives working on murder investigations, even in recent times, it often appears as if the main characters operate in a bubble where there are no incident rooms staffed by many, no investigation teams and very little, if any, paperwork or statements created. The reality is far from this. A huge machine kicks in as soon as a suspicious death or murder occurs. Quite rightly too, as these represent the most high-profile and serious of investigations undertaken by police officers.

Kevin Moore

However, the point I wish to make at this stage is simply this. The public are fascinated with the act of murder and its investigation. Often, it is portrayed in fiction as a triumph of good over evil, in relation to the police investigation. This makes for great story lines and, dare I say, an increasing depiction of the most bizarre circumstances, some almost beyond belief! As I go through my book, I intend to highlight the reality of murder investigation in all its guises. However, to get to that point, it is worthy of consideration to discuss why we, the public, are so fascinated by murder, almost to the point of obsession.

Murder is the most brutal of crimes. It involves violence, often gratuitous, and is the ultimate taboo. Why, then, are so many people obsessed with the subject? The public appear to be insatiable when it comes to this most ultimate of crimes. Their obsession with the facts of murder manifests itself in wanting to know who did it? How and Why? Did the person involved know what they were doing? Was it premeditated or a spur of the moment crime of passion? It is arguably the case that people have always been fascinated by extreme behaviour and crime, especially murder. Nowadays, there are many more avenues to find out about murder or other crime than ever before.

There is a whole plethora of sources for people to access to satisfy their interests, ranging from crime novels, fictional films and TV shows, to 'real crime' programmes and ventures looking at previous cases. Cases involving murder are incorporated in some of the most read books, films and TV programmes. Indeed, a journalist acquaintance of mine confirmed that police-related documentaries always attract some of the highest audiences. Therefore, such material is highly prized and sought after.

From fictional depictions, such as Inspector Morse or Luther, to true crime stories, such as the Moors Murderers Ian Brady and Myra Hindley, the serial killers Fred and Rose

REAL MURDER INVESTIGATIONS

West, and Dr Harold Shipman, we seem obsessed by the calculated killings of the world's most deranged men and women. TV audiences have gorged themselves on programmes such as Netflix's *Making a Murderer*. Murder is a major source of entertainment, with the killers involved in the most incomprehensible savagery gaining most attention. Crime drama mysteries involving a particular murder, whether in books, TV shows, documentaries or news broadcasts - the public are hooked on them! Perhaps it is an opportunity to see the wrongs of the world put right which often doesn't happen in the 'real world'. Could it be the case that we inwardly gain pleasure at some other individual's misfortune? More than one person has told me they enjoy watching *Eastenders*, because the characters are always unhappy and experience problems and issues, and therefore they feel better about their own lives! In the days of capital punishment and public hangings, there was never a shortage of 'witnesses' to such events.

Academics have argued that behaviour that a normal person wouldn't consider being involved in, such as murder or mass killings, interests people. There is a built-in fascination in extremities of human behaviour because murder is an act beyond the comprehension of most people. Similarly, it has been argued that the media plays a significant role in helping to increase this fascination. Murder potentially becomes an avenue for the offender to gain fame/infamy. A crime narrative begins with a problem and it has a quest for knowledge and truth. At the end, there is hopefully some sense of understanding as to what happened.

Thankfully the vast majority of us do not approve of the actions of those who commit murder, but we still wish to look. We want to see who died and how, and often we forensically linger on the death. The TV show *Silent Witness* continues to thrive after many years and attracts huge

Kevin Moore

audiences. Even so-called soap operas attempt to spice up their story lines occasionally with a juicy murder, and viewers lap it up! We are horrified with killing and death, but we still cannot avoid looking, it would seem. Consider the so called 'rubber necking' that takes place at the scenes of road traffic crashes. There are good examples of the creation of the most bizarre and far-fetched in TV drama shows such as *Luther*. However, the viewing figures are always amongst the highest. Crime Fiction sections in book shops are the most highly read. Put another way, therefore, killing appears to sell.

Academics have also pointed out that, in order to almost justify our wish to be involved in murder, we want to take the time to empathise and sympathise with those who have lost their loved ones. Similarly, in an effort to ensure that we distance ourselves from the perpetrators of murder, we dehumanise them. We are arguably helped in this by the media who, when describing individuals involved, use terms such as 'monster' or 'evil'. Therefore, the more offenders are dehumanised, the easier it becomes to distance ourselves from them. This assists in answering questions such as – 'Why did they do it?' or 'Could I do that?' 'Was there nothing/no one who could have stopped this happening?'

Murders, particularly those involving serial killers, tantalise people, much as traffic accidents, train crashes and other disaster scenarios do. Some have argued that the public has an inbuilt fixation with violence and calamity. It may also give a jolt of adrenalin which can become addictive. This is a little like watching horror movies because we enjoy an element of fear. Arguably, this can be classified as the most basic and powerful emotion within all of us. This can best be highlighted in those individuals who tend towards thrill seeking in its many guises. Therefore, viewing such matters could generally be described as some form of guilty pleasure. There are few, if any, heroes these days and in real

REAL MURDER INVESTIGATIONS

life, there are few, if indeed any, happy endings. However, murder does exert a weird fascination.

There is no doubt that an element of interest arises from the fact that most people thankfully lead relatively mundane lives. So murder brings an element of excitement, whether in the real world or the fictional one. Becoming involved breaks the monotony for some. I have seen this at first hand with friends, not involved in policing, who can't wait to question me about cases. I believe that this, for them, is because murder is not a part of the real world, as fortunately the huge majority of us will never experience it directly.

The fascination with murder is enhanced if a high-profile personality is involved, for example, the cases of OJ Simpson and Oscar Pistorius. Both trials were followed avidly and one can foresee that, if ever court trials were broadcast in this country, it is likely that the viewing figures would be similarly high.

The public are often particularly obsessed with serial killers. Some writers have described the reasons for this as follows. Firstly, they are extreme in their brutality and so unnatural in their behaviour that people are drawn to such cases out of intense curiosity. Secondly, they generally kill randomly, choosing victims based on personal attraction or opportunities presented to them. This factor potentially makes everyone a possible victim. Thirdly, serial killers are prolific and insatiable which means they kill many people over a period of years, rather than killing one person in a single, impulsive act. Fourthly, their behaviour is seemingly inexplicable and lacking a coherent motive, such as jealousy or rage. They are driven by inner demons that they themselves may not comprehend. People are fascinated by serial killers because they are constantly wrestling with the question 'Why?'

There seems to be a particular fascination with women who kill. There have been many documentaries, real crime programmes and fictional depictions of female killers. Questions are asked as to what drives a woman to commit murder and there almost seems to be a particular revulsion that a woman can have committed such a crime.

Such cases seem to create their own public obsession. This even goes to the point where, at a woman's trial, media coverage will often include completely irrelevant matters, such as how the woman looked and what she was wearing, including make-up etc. Why does this happen? Often the media coverage will focus more on lurid details than in the case of a man on trial. Sometimes, there is suggested that the impulse to kill was linked with a voracious sexual appetite. There have even been attempts to show that a woman is deadlier than a man in such cases! However, it is more likely that the fascination with a female killer is more because they are a rarity than for any other reason. Men are deadlier than woman, statistically, at least.

A good example is the case involving the Moors Murderers Ian Brady and Myra Hindley. Whilst, arguably at least, they were both equally culpable, if not more so in the case of Brady, Hindley has always attracted more attention as a witch personified – 'the most evil woman in Britain'.

Female murderers are more likely to cause a sensation because they transgress the 'norms' of their gender. A certain level of aggression in men seems to be expected and may even be seen as a quality. Women in contrast are seen as carers and nurturers, rather than being able to hurt and kill. A case in point involves the American Amanda Knox. She was accused of murdering British student Meredith Kercher in Italy. Great emphasis was placed on her being sexually promiscuous and an 'enchanting witch' who was into kinky sex. After her subsequent acquittal, Knox stated, 'People love monsters and so when they get the chance, they want to see them. They want the reassurance of knowing who the bad people are, and it's not them.' Women may be

REAL MURDER INVESTIGATIONS

less prone to commit murder but that does not mean they automatically possess some quality of innocent, natural caregivers.

Women are responsible for most infant murders in Britain and between 10-20% of sexual offences against children. This is quite a small figure in comparison with men. However, it is often portrayed as somehow being more horrific.

The criminal barrister Helena Kennedy, who represented Myra Hindley, said it was right that Hindley should never be released. She also felt it was less likely that women will be forgiven for their crimes. In addition to the rules of the Criminal Justice system, she believed that women were subjected to the rules of womanhood. She is quoted as saying, 'We expect women to be better than men – there is that unspoken thing – that we are shocked when women do terrible things.'

Finally, there is often a public fascination with the police investigation e.g. were there many suspects or was it someone acting alone and in isolation? Were the clues obvious or subtle? Did the investigation require science or logic? Did the detective involved in the case have to use insight, acute powers of detective ability or just hard work? Was the offender the usual obvious candidate or was it a person that nobody would ever have suspected? Finally, when the investigation is over, did the right person get convicted?

By way of introduction to the main part of this book, I have tried to show why the subject of murder has become as prevalent as it has in the lives of the public. This is due to many reasons, including a general fascination with murder and death, which is arguably within us all. Some of the reasons for this are undoubtedly due to the type of murder involved, or the age and gender of the victim. Additionally, I have outlined the rise in media coverage and its depiction of murder and murderers. Also, as has been discussed previously, there has been a huge increase in the number of books, TV shows, films and real crime murder documentaries over the years, both fiction and non-fiction. This does not appear to have threatened to flood the market. Indeed, it would appear that there still remains a thirst for such coverage. The public appears insatiable. Arguably, it potentially provides a form of escapism.

I have already touched on the implications of the fictional portrayal, as opposed to the truth of murder investigation. The stark reality is that murder investigations involve a huge system and process being put in place, made up of a large number of individuals and teams who possess particular expertise in different areas. These include:

Senior Investigation Officer
Deputy Senior Investigation Officer
The major incident room and its staffing, including the Incident Room Manager and other senior detectives acting as receivers and action allocators, HOLMES (Home Office Large Major Enquiry System), Indexers and Analysts and Typists
Scenes of Crime teams, including photography
Search teams
House to House teams
Outside Enquiry teams (Detectives)
Investigative interviewers for key witnesses and suspects
Family Liaison Officers
Exhibits Officers
Disclosure Officers
Intelligence development officers
Media relations staff
The completion of **Community Impact Assessments** and their links to Neighbourhood Policing

REAL MURDER INVESTIGATIONS

This will be covered in far greater detail in later chapters. However, I wish to make some observations at this point as regards the reality of murder and its investigation. There is inevitably a relatively glamorous portrayal of detectives involved in murder investigation, both within the media and fictionally. However, this tends to defy reality. Murder investigations in the real world are high profile, and quite properly are still, in the main, given a high priority in terms of media attention. From a practical point of view, in terms of investigation, they are far from glamorous.

From an investigator's point of view, there is a professional wish to achieve a positive outcome for the victims and their families. That is the case, even if the victim is a known criminal. It makes no difference to the investigator. They always want to achieve a positive outcome. For every family of a victim, murder is a tragedy. This is the only practical thing the police can achieve, bearing in mind the circumstances. Depending on the type of murder, there is huge public as well as media interest. Speaking as a former Senior Investigating Officer (SIO), the thirst for investigation updates, especially in the early stages of the investigation, is on occasions incredible.

The most difficult of such investigations present the most severe professional challenges. However, detectives usually welcome these opportunities. They present those involved with what has always been seen, in policing terms, as the greatest reason for being *(raison d'être)*. As written in the Homicide Investigator's Creed at the start of this book, there is no greater privilege than to be tasked with investigating the death of another human being.

However, it would be fair to point out that such intensity brings its own issues. For that reason, murder, and serious crime investigation more generally, is not necessarily what all police officers aspire to be involved in. There are many personal pressures. As an example, especially in the early stages of a new investigation, there is a need to work extremely long hours, including periods without any days off. The more difficult and high profile the case, the more likely this is to occur. Therefore, an understanding spouse or partner is a 'must have'! Personally, I loved these challenges at whatever level/rank I was involved. I relished the levels of commitment expected. Being regularly on call and being contacted in the middle of the night never fazed me. I recall the early days of hands-free mobile phones. This was a great advance because suddenly, as an SIO on my way to a scene following a call out, I could start to put things in place, whilst still making my way there. Leading a murder investigation is, however, not for the faint hearted! You are everyone's friend when things are going well. However, when events prove difficult, you soon find out who your true friends are, even within the organisation itself!

Throughout this book, I have used case studies to emphasise particular points or issues. Quite deliberately, this is not a memoire of all the cases with which I have been involved over the years. There are far too many to include here. I have tried to be selective, to include not only the most relevant to highlight key issues, but also those which I believe to be the most interesting.

I will end this particular chapter with some statistics regarding murder in England and Wales. Fortunately, murder in the UK is still rare, relatively speaking. In the 1960s, homicides were between 300-350 per annum. This rose gradually until a peak in 2002-2003 where the statistics involving Harold Shipman appear, artificially raising the numbers to 1,047. Up until 2018, the numbers dropped to 533 in 2013-2014, before rising again to 736 for the year 2017-2018 (for counting purposes, years operate from 1st April to 31st March, rather than calendar years).

There are many things to bear in mind with these statistics. Firstly, there has been a considerable increase in

REAL MURDER INVESTIGATIONS

population since the 1960s and so this is likely to increase proportionately the commission of such offences. Also, where multiple deaths occur, arising out of one incident or investigation, this leads to what can amount to a short-term artificial inflation of the figures e.g. Harold Shipman, as well as instances of terrorism where multiple deaths occur. However, the reality is that murder has increased considerably during the past decade, and the increase in knife and gun-related murders in London and other major cities has been considerable.

It is also important to put things into perspective. Generally speaking, offences of murder are still rare. To provide some context, in a county the size of Sussex with a population of around 1.5 million, we used to expect 15-20 murders per annum. Fortunately, instances of serial killings are very rare and indeed, there was no such occasion in Sussex during my 40 years of service from 1978-2018. Therefore, in order to discuss issues regarding such matters, my case studies include just a couple of cases with which I have had less direct involvement. One of these involves the case of Levi Bellfield, the killer of Milly Dowler, which was an investigation led by Surrey Police and was the subject of a review carried out by Sussex Police which I led. Bellfield was previously convicted of the murders of two other young women and the attempted murder of a third. I shall also look at Operation Anagram, the nationally-led investigation which looked into the possible involvement of Peter Tobin in other murders, after his conviction for the murders of three women. Both cases are referred to, later on.

However, before moving onto the major chapters of the book, I will start with legal definitions and their meanings. These are important because it gives some clarity to the non-police reader as to what actually constitutes murder, and the difference between this and manslaughter, as well as potential legal defences.

CHAPTER 2
Legal Definitions and Defences in Law

When discussing murder, especially for those readers who are not involved with the law, it will undoubtedly be of interest to understand what murder actually is and what defences there are to murder, and, at the same time, learn the differences between murder and manslaughter.

The definition of murder, and just as importantly its interpretation, is not necessarily as straightforward as it may seem. Indeed, even some senior detectives have difficulty understanding the various nuances on occasions!

In its strictest terms, murder is the unlawful killing of another human without justification or valid excuse, especially the unlawful killing of another human being with malice aforethought. This state of mind may, depending upon the jurisdiction, distinguish murder from any other form of unlawful homicide such as manslaughter.

Manslaughter is a killing committed without malice, brought about by reasonable provocation or diminished capacity. Involuntary manslaughter, where it is recognised as such, is a killing that lacks all but the weakest/thinnest guilty intent or is reckless.

Murder is, of course, recognised in most civilisations as the most serious of crimes and therefore is punishable with life or very lengthy prison sentences, or, as is still the case in some countries, with the death penalty.

The Common Law definition states that murder is when a person of sound mind and discretion, unlawfully kills any reasonable creature in being under the King's (Queen's) peace, with malice aforethought, either express or implied.

Unlawful – means that murder is distinguished from killings that are carried out within the boundaries of law

REAL MURDER INVESTIGATIONS

such as:
- Capital punishment
- Justified self defence
- The killing of enemy combatants by lawful combatants, as well as collateral damage to non-combatants during a war

Killing – At common law, life ended with cardio-pulmonary arrest i.e. the total cessation of blood circulation and respiration. With advances in medical technology, courts have adopted irreversible cessation of brain function as marking the end of life.

Criminal act or omission – killing can be committed by an act or an omission.

Of a human – This element presents the issue of when life begins. At common law, a foetus is not a human being. Life begins when the foetus enters the world and draws breath.

By another human being – In early common law, suicide was considered to be murder. The requirement that the person be killed by someone other than the perpetrator later excluded suicide from the definition of murder.

With malice aforethought – Originally, this term carried its everyday meaning i.e. a deliberate and premeditated (prior intent) killing of another, motivated by ill will. Murder necessarily required that an appreciable time pass between the formation and execution of the intent to kill. The courts later broadened the scope of murder by eliminating the requirement of actual premeditation and deliberation, as well as true malice. All that is now required for malice aforethought to exist is that the offender acts with one of the following states of mind to constitute malice:

1. Intent to kill
2. Intent to inflict grievous (really serious) bodily harm, short of death

3. Reckless indifference to an unjustifiably high risk to human life (abandoned or malignant heart – a technical term referring to inner feelings at the time of the act itself)
4. Intent to commit a dangerous felony

Under 1 above, the deadly weapon rule applies. Therefore, the defendant has to intentionally use a deadly weapon or instrument, such as but not limited to: guns, knives, deadly toxins, chemicals or gases and even vehicles, when intentionally used to harm one or more victims.

Under 3, the killing must result from the defendant's conduct involving a reckless indifference to human life and a conscious disregard of an unreasonable risk of death or serious bodily injury.

Under 4, the felony involved must be an inherently dangerous one such as burglary, arson, rape, robbery or kidnapping. Importantly, however, the underlying felony cannot be a lesser offence such as assault, otherwise all criminal homicides would be murder, as all are felonies because an assault is an integral element of murder.

In this country, unlike some such as the US, we do not recognise so called *degrees of murder e.g. first or second degree*. Additionally, in such jurisdictions, similar types of murder may be differentiated through a specific intent to kill, premeditation or deliberation.

Exclusion or defences

Killing of enemy combatants, who have not surrendered in accordance with lawful orders in war, is also not considered murder. However, illegal killings within a war may constitute murder or homicidal war crimes.

Self-defence - acting in self-defence or in defence of another - is generally accepted as legal justification for the killing of a person when, in other circumstances, this may well constitute murder. However, a self-defence killing might be considered to be manslaughter, if the killer establishes control of the situation before the killing took place. In the case of self-defence, the correct term is *'justifiable homicide'*.

Unlawful killings without malice aforethought are considered to be manslaughter.

Provocation can be a partial defence to a charge of murder, which acts by converting what would have been murder into manslaughter. This is known as *'voluntary manslaughter'* which is more severe than *'involuntary manslaughter'*.

Accidental killings are considered to be homicides. Depending on the circumstances, these may or may not be considered criminal offences. They are often considered to be manslaughter. Such circumstances are relevant to the murder of Jane Longhurst by Graham Coutts which I shall be dealing with later.

Suicide does not constitute murder in this country but *assisting a suicide* could, in certain circumstances, constitute murder. There is still much discussion and debate about the issue of the guilt of somebody assisting a person to end their life when they are suffering from incurable or terminal illnesses. Currently, any person involved in such action, even if a doctor, will be guilty of assisting a suicide or could even be guilty of murder. I do not intend to explore this further here as this could well be a subject for discussion in its own right.

Mitigating Circumstances

Conditions which affect the 'balance of the mind' can be regarded as mitigating circumstances. This means that a person may be found guilty of manslaughter on the basis of 'diminished responsibility', rather than murder. This is the case if the defendant can prove they were suffering from a condition that affected their judgement at the time. Cases involving a person suffering from depression, post-traumatic stress disorder and the side effects of prescribed medication are examples of conditions that may be taken into account when assessing responsibility.

Insanity – Mental disorder may excuse the person involved from undergoing the stress of a trial as to liability. Usually, sociopathy and other personality disorders are not legally considered to amount to insanity, because they are believed to be the result of free will in many societies. Following a pre-trial hearing to determine the extent of any reported disorder, the defence of 'not guilty by reason of insanity' may be used to gain a not guilty verdict. There are two elements to this defence. Firstly, that the defendant had a serious mental illness, disease or defect. Secondly, that the defendant's mental condition, at the time of the killing, rendered him or her unable to determine right from wrong or that what they were doing was wrong.

A criminal defendant is often presented with the option of pleading 'not guilty by reason of insanity'. A finding of insanity results in a not guilty verdict, although the defendant is usually referred to mandatory clinical treatment, rather than prison, and placed in a state-run institution where they can be kept for many years, until they are certified as fit to be released back into the community.

Post-natal depression – This is recognised as a potential mitigating factor in cases involving infanticide. The penalty for mothers who kill their children of up to one year of age can be decreased in certain circumstances when, at the time of the act or omission, the balance of the mother's mind was disturbed by reason of her not having fully recovered from the effect of giving birth to the child, or by reason of the effect.

Diminished responsibility/capacity – diminished responsibility may be a defence to murder and lead to a finding of guilty to manslaughter, in certain circumstances. These occasions relate to legal doctrine that absolves an accused person of part of the liability for their criminal act, if they suffer from such abnormality of mind as to substantially impair their responsibility in committing, or being a party to, an alleged criminal offence.

Cases involving diminished responsibility are most likely those with a 'domestic' element to them e.g. those involving husbands, wives and partners. Mainly spur of the moment actions, they may also involve what have been referred to as 'crimes of passion'. It has been recognised, more recently, that such findings may also be relevant when they involve women who have been the victims of domestic abuse.

The most used example in terms of diminished responsibility, however, are those cases involving defendants who acted whilst the 'balance of their mind was disturbed'. In other words, where they were suffering from such a defect in their mind, that this led to them killing the deceased person.

Sentencing and Aggravating or Mitigating factors

It is also helpful for the reader to understand matters which affect sanctions if an individual is found guilty.

Where the offender is 21 or over at the time of the offence, and the court takes the view that the murder is so serious that the offender should spend the rest of their life in prison, a 'whole life order' is the appropriate starting point. The early release provisions in Section 28 of the Crime (Sentences) Act 1997 will then not apply. Such an order should only be specified where the court considers that the seriousness of the offence is exceptionally high.

Such cases include:
1. the murder of two or more persons where each murder involves a substantial degree of

premeditation, the abduction of the victim, or sexual or sadistic conduct;
2. the murder of a child if involving the abduction of the child or sexual or sadistic motivation;
3. a murder done for the purpose of advancing a political, religious or ideological cause; or
4. a murder by an offender previously convicted of murder.

Where the offence is not so serious as to warrant a whole life order, but the seriousness of the offence is particularly high, the appropriate starting point is 30 years. The following examples are given:
1. the murder of a police or prison officer in the course of his/her duty;
2. a murder involving the use of a firearm or explosive;
3. a murder done for gain (in the course of a robbery or burglary, or done for payment – so called contract killings);
4. a murder intended to obstruct or interfere with the course of justice;
5. a murder involving sexual or sadistic conduct;
6. the murder of two or more persons; or
7. a murder that is racially or religiously aggravated, or aggravated by sexual orientation.

Where the offender took a knife or other weapon to the scene, intending to commit any offence, or have it available to use as a weapon, and used that knife or other weapon in committing the murder, the normal starting point is 25 years. This increased minimum term does not apply in relation to a life sentence imposed for an offence of murder committed before 2nd March 2010.

For all other offences, the appropriate starting point is 15 years.

Having set a starting point, the court must take into account any aggravating or mitigating factors, to the extent

REAL MURDER INVESTIGATIONS

that it has not allowed for them in its choice of starting point.

Consideration of aggravating or mitigating factors may result in a minimum term of any length, (whatever the starting point), or in making a whole life order.

Aggravating factors that may be relevant include:
1. a significant degree of planning or premeditation;
2. the victim was vulnerable because of age or disability;
3. mental or physical suffering inflicted on the victim before death;
4. the abuse of a position of trust;
5. the use of duress or threats against another person to facilitate the commission of the offence;
6. the victim was providing a public service or performing a public duty; and
7. concealment, destruction or dismemberment of the body.

Mitigating factors include:
1. an intention to cause serious bodily harm rather than kill;
2. lack of premeditation;
3. the offender suffers from a mental disorder or disability (not falling within Section 2(1) of the Homicide Act 1957) which lowered their degree of culpability;
4. the offender was provoked in a way not amounting to a defence of provocation;
5. the offender acted to any extent in self-defence;
6. a belief by the offender that the murder was an act of mercy; and
7. the age of the offender

The court should also consider any previous convictions, whether the offence was committed on bail and if the offender pleaded guilty.

The court should take into account any period the offender has spent on remand in connection with the offence or a related offence. The offender will get no credit for time served on remand unless it is taken into account when setting the minimum term. The court should normally subtract the time for which the offender was remanded, from the punitive period it would otherwise impose, in order to reach the minimum term.

People often have difficulty understanding why a murder charge is changed to one of manslaughter. Additionally, it may be confusing as to why a judge, when summing up, in appropriate cases addresses the jury as regards the law on manslaughter, giving the option of a finding of not guilty to murder but guilty of manslaughter. Of course, it doesn't necessarily prevent a jury from finding a defendant guilty of murder. It just means that, if they are not satisfied that the necessary level of intent is present to be guilty of either murder or grievous bodily harm with intent, they have the alternative to find the defendant guilty of manslaughter.

The following examples of decisions, made through what is known as 'case law', are included to assist understanding. These are past cases which serve to assist judges and barristers in applying the law. Such individuals can quote from these cases during court proceedings. As well as hopefully being helpful, they are individually interesting. To assist the reader, the term 'R' means 'Regina', as in the Queen/King. 'DPP' is the abbreviation for the 'Director of Public Prosecution's. 'LJ' means 'Lord Justice'.

Abnormality of mind

R v Byrne [1960] 2 Queens Bench Division 396. The defendant had strangled a young woman and then mutilated her body. He claimed he was subject to an irresistible impulse because of violent perverted sexual desires. These had overcome him ever since he was a boy. There was evidence that he was a sexual psychopath and could exercise little control over his actions. The defence of diminished responsibility was rejected by the trial judge, and the defendant was convicted of murder. The Court of Appeal allowed the defendant's appeal on the basis that the trial judge had been wrong to exclude, from the scope of the defence, situations where a defendant was simply unable to exercise any self-control over his actions. (This would cover the irresistible impulse situation.)

Lord Parker CJ stated: 'Abnormality of mind - means a state of mind so different from that of ordinary human beings that the reasonable man would term it abnormal. It appears to us to be wide enough to cover the mind's activities in all its aspects, not only the perception of physical acts and matters, and the ability to form a rational judgement whether an act is right or wrong, but also the ability to exercise will power to control physical acts in accordance with that rational judgement.'

His Lordship pointed out that, whether the defendant was suffering from any 'abnormality of mind' is a question for the jury. On this question, medical evidence is important, but the jury are entitled to take into consideration all the evidence, including acts or statements of the defendant, and his demeanour. They are not bound to accept the medical evidence, if there is other material before them which, in their judgement, conflicts with and outweighs it. The cause of the abnormality of mind does, however, seem to be a matter to be determined on expert evidence.

Diminished Responsibility and Intoxication

R v Gittens [1984] QB (Queens Bench Division) 698. The defendant suffered from depression and had been in hospital. On a visit home, he had an argument with his wife and clubbed her to death. He then raped and killed his stepdaughter. He had been drinking and taking prescribed drugs. The Court of Appeal suggested that, where the jury

had to deal with both diminished responsibility and intoxication, they should be directed to consider:
1. whether the defendant would have killed as he did without having been intoxicated, and if the answer to that was yes,
2. whether he would have been suffering from diminished responsibility when he did so.

Section 2(2) states clearly that the burden of proving the defence rests upon the defendant. Given that the standard of proof which the defendant has to achieve is the balance of probabilities, he will have to obtain cogent medical evidence as to his condition.

If successfully pleaded, the defence avoids the imposition of a mandatory life sentence and enables the court to give whatever sentence it thinks appropriate. This can include a hospital order under Section 37 of the Mental Health Act 1983, thus ensuring treatment, not punishment, in appropriate cases. (This is now imposed in approximately one-third of diminished responsibility cases.)

Provocation

R v Doughty [1986]. The defendant had killed his baby and wanted to argue that he had been provoked by the child's persistent crying. On appeal, it was held to be a misdirection for the trial judge to tell the jury that the persistent crying of a 17-day-old baby could not constitute provocation, and therefore the Appeal Court quashed the murder conviction and substituted a conviction for manslaughter. The jury should have been directed to consider how the reasonable man would have responded.

The first element of the provocation test is subjective – the requirement that the defendant must be shown to have actually lost his self-control. If there is evidence that his actions were premeditated, or that he had been able to compose himself between the provocation and the killing, then this defence cannot be left to the jury to determine.

REAL MURDER INVESTIGATIONS

Where there is a time gap between provocation and killing ('cooling time'), the defendant may encounter difficulties in trying to establish the defence of provocation:

R v Ibrams and Gregory (1981). The defendants and a young woman had been terrorised and bullied by the deceased, over a period of time, but the last act occurred on 7th October. On 10th October, they devised a plan which involved the woman enticing the deceased to her bed, whereupon the defendants would burst in and attack him. The plan was carried out on 12th October. The defendants were convicted of murder and on appeal, it was held that the judge was right to rule that there was no evidence of loss of self-control. Lawton LJ expressed the view that the time gap between the last act of provocation and the killing refuted any evidence that it had been carried out by the defendants suffering from a sudden and temporary loss of self-control, as envisaged by Devlin J in Duffy [1949].

The Court of Appeal recently made it clear that a defence of provocation can succeed if there is a series of incidents over time which drove the person to murder.

The killing of the Reverend Ronald Glazebrook by the defendant Christopher Hunnisett, which I will discuss later, involved an element of provocation.

The reasonable man test

Having decided that the defendant was provoked, the jury must then decide whether a reasonable man would have acted as the defendant did – the objective test. The reasonable man is attributed with the defendant's particular characteristics which might be relevant to the provocation:

DPP v Camplin [1978]. The defendant was a 15-year-old boy who, having been buggered by the deceased, was then taunted by him. The defendant killed the deceased by hitting him over the head with a heavy frying pan. He was convicted of murder following a direction by the trial judge to the jury that they were to judge him by the standards of the reasonable adult, not a reasonable 15-year-old boy. The Court of Appeal allowed the defendant's appeal on the basis that the more subjective test, which took account of the defendant's age, should have been applied. This was endorsed by the House of Lords.

Lord Diplock gave the following definition of the reasonable man: '... the "reasonable man" has never been confined to the adult male. It means an ordinary person of either sex, not exceptionally excitable or pugnacious, but possessed of such powers of self-control as everyone is entitled to expect that his fellow citizens will exercise in society as it is today.'

The judge should, according to Lord Diplock, explain to the jury that the reasonable man referred to is a person having the power of self-control to be expected of an ordinary person of the sex and age of the defendant, but in all other respects showing such of the defendant's characteristics as they think would affect the gravity of the provocation to him. The question is not merely whether such a person would, in the circumstances, be provoked to lose his self-control but also whether he would react to the provocation as the defendant did.

Hence, whilst the age and sex of the defendant would always be attributed to the reasonable man, other characteristics such as racial origin, or physical peculiarity, would only be considered to the extent that they were relevant. Thus, in the present case, the reasonable man would be the reasonable 15-year-old, as the defendant's youth was a relevant characteristic. As certain characteristics, such as intoxication or excitability, would be ignored for policy reasons, the defendant's drunkenness was irrelevant.

The House of Lords recently had to decide whether the judge should exclude from the jury's consideration, any of the defendant's characteristics and past behaviour (if the

REAL MURDER INVESTIGATIONS

taunts are directed at such behaviour), which, in the judge's view, are inconsistent with the concept of a reasonable man. In other words, if the defendant's actions (taunts) are viewed as being totally unreasonable in any given set of circumstances.

If the defendant induces the provocation by some act of his own, the defence will still be available.

These examples hopefully assist understanding and in particular why certain circumstances may mean that what originally seemed to be murder may later result in a verdict of manslaughter or acceptance of a legal defence.

CHAPTER 3

The Professionalisation of Murder Investigation Over The Years

In writing this next chapter, my intention is not to say that in years gone by, police response to murder has been less than professional or that the capabilities of those investigating such cases were less. Indeed, far from it. Over the years, there have been many distinguished murder investigators and certainly in my early years as a junior detective, I learned from some of the best.

However, what is not in doubt is that professionalisation has increased. This didn't start to happen until the 1960s when provincial police forces began to run murder investigations for themselves. Up to then, the Metropolitan Police (Met) would send out one of their senior investigators, supported by one or two junior detectives, to take charge of such enquiries. The local force would provide the necessary resources but were directed by the senior detective from the Met. Forces outside London therefore 'Called in the Yard' to undertake the investigation of these high-profile crimes. In 1992/1993, writing the dissertation for my degree, I advocated the creation of dedicated homicide investigation teams. I actually and ironically entitled it 'Call in the Yard', to reflect the fact that we needed to take the next step forward in terms of progress.

Until fairly recently, most forces outside the Metropolitan forces, did not have dedicated murder teams. Indeed, in Sussex, it was almost ten years after I completed my dissertation that Sussex moved towards this. Most forces after the 1960s, including Sussex, appointed a senior detective from within the force to lead the investigation and they pulled together a team of detectives from the local area

REAL MURDER INVESTIGATIONS

and beyond, to assist them. This was hugely cumbersome and invariably meant that the Senior Investigating Officer (SIO) spent a good deal of time, calling in favours from colleagues across the force as nobody wanted to willingly give up their staff to assist.

Today, the whole approach has been professionalised, originally by the Met, which was then inevitably followed, to a greater or lesser extent, by the country's provincial forces. Every force now has its own 'stand-alone' murder investigation team, although some forces have collaborated with neighbouring forces in order to benefit from potential economies of scale. This has been a hugely significant development and, in many cases, was speeded along after mistakes were made during such investigations.

Looking back to the 1960s, even though forces were starting to run their own homicide investigations, there was still the opportunity to request assistance from the Met. On 6th May 1967, in Sussex, a local schoolboy, Keith Lyon, aged 12, was stabbed to death. His body was found on a bridleway running between Ovingdean and Woodingdean, on the outskirts of Brighton. Despite the best efforts of the local force, led by Detective Chief Superintendent Jim Marshall, the case remains unsolved to this day. At that time, there were calls for the Met to take over the investigation. This did not happen, and it has to be said that it is very unlikely they would have been any more successful than the local officers were. Jim Marshall was considered one of the finest detectives of his day and if anyone could solve the case, he could. It also needs to be remembered that until 1967/1968, there were many more police forces than there are today, and they were much smaller. Indeed, there were several hundred. This was before amalgamations were implemented. At the time, for instance, the county of Sussex was made up of five forces - the two county forces of East and West Sussex, as well as the three boroughs of Brighton,

Eastbourne and Hastings. Therefore, forces were very small in comparison with the 43 that exist now and were commensurately lighter in terms of numbers as well as expertise. Often, these smaller forces had to 'borrow' particular specialisms from their neighbours.

Interestingly, the Lyon case was reopened by Sussex Police in 2006 as a 'Cold Case' or 'Unresolved Case'. Based on DNA evidence found at the scene, two men, who were youngsters at the time of the murder, were actually arrested but not charged due to insufficient evidence. Of course, such advances in forensic science were still unknown in the 1960s and indeed for many years afterwards. The investigation remains open.

Right up to this day, the vast majority of murders are solved. This is mainly for two reasons. Firstly, most murder victims know their attacker and may even be in some form of relationship with the offender. Secondly, due to the high-profile nature of such cases, considerable resources are quite properly dedicated to such investigations. No stone is left unturned.

Developments in Forensic Science have, of course, been considerable over the years. Looking at old footage as well as fictional depiction of such cases, things were positively archaic compared to today. However, it has to be said that the capabilities of individual detectives are likely to have been as sound then as they are now. Like advances in forensic science, what has without doubt changed is the degree of professionalisation involving the investigation of murder. Much of what is done now is based on what has been learned from days gone by, both good and bad. A good example of this is the way in which law enforcement now deals with the issue of preventing cross contamination of exhibits and scenes bearing potential scientific evidence. Cross contamination was virtually unheard of until the 1980s. This is due in no small part to the developments and

REAL MURDER INVESTIGATIONS

sensitivity of forensic science techniques in terms of the retrieval and interpretation of such evidence.

I will be returning to this later when I consider the double murder case of Nicola Fellows and Karen Hadaway, at the hands of the recently convicted Russell Bishop. In the first trial in 1987, Russell Bishop's defence team placed great emphasis on the potential for contamination of forensic evidence.

The benefit of hindsight is a wonderful thing, as we know. However, if we learn from that hindsight and any mistakes from the past, then that must be a good thing. The ways of investigating murder are no different in this regard. We owe the way we do things now, and the advances made, to the legacy of those investigators who went before us.

Training and accreditation are among the greatest developments. In terms of homicide investigators, in the past, it was pretty much a case of learning from those who were operating in such roles. Whilst this is no bad thing, and certainly, in my own case, assisted me greatly, investigators at all levels can now access hard skills training. Every element in a murder investigation team is handled by individuals who have been properly trained and who have then had the opportunity to put the skills learned into practice, in order to build their levels of professionalism.

Whilst we acknowledge the advances made in relation to the elements that make up a murder investigation team, we need to remember that many of these concepts existed even in days gone by. A good example of this is the Murder or Major Incident Room. This is made up of numerous individuals, both police officers and police staff, who are trained and experienced in the elements required to properly run an Incident Room. Additionally, nowadays, the whole system is computerised through HOLMES (Home Office Large Major Enquiry System). This system has been refined considerably over the years and whilst all such investigations now have the potential to be linked across the whole country, as all forces use this system, this was a luxury that was not present until the mid-1980s. Even then, the computer systems were 'stand-alone' and therefore there was no opportunity to link investigations as there is now.

Of course, HOLMES is the legacy of the so-called Yorkshire Ripper investigation involving the serial killer Peter Sutcliffe. His name featured seven times during the course of that investigation and he was spoken to by the police more than once before his arrest. However, the significance of this was not appreciated, simply because the officers involved were unable to make the necessary evidential links. This automatically happens now because of the availability, through HOLMES, of free text searching and what is known as indexing.

Everything in the early days was recorded on index cards which were retained in what was known as a carousel, due to the circular shape of the filing mechanism. Whilst there were attempts to cross reference material indexed on cards, this relied on individuals doing this through their own thought processes. Just imagine the size of the Sutcliffe case, taking into account the volume of murders. How on earth could any card system be foolproof? HOLMES undertakes this automatically, simply because of the way the programme has been designed, which requires inputting in a particular format. It means that all documentation is handled in line with strict rules and conventions, enabling ease of cross referencing and linking.

There was little or no training in those early days for officers performing those functions, and of course, all roles, except for the typing of statements and reports, were completed by police officers. Today, those with the necessary skills are the ones performing the different roles within the incident room and these can often be police staff. For some time now, only those roles requiring a detective

REAL MURDER INVESTIGATIONS

are filled by police officers. These include those individuals responsible for reading the incoming statements and other documentation, and then raising what are called 'actions' to be carried out by detectives working as part of the 'outside enquiry team'.

In order to ensure that there is strict adherence to laid down systems, processes and protocol, MIRSAP (Major Incident Room Standardised Administrative Procedures) was developed. This outlines, in clear terms, the roles and responsibilities of the staff working in a Major Incident Room and is designed to bring about a consistency in approach.

There are many other roles and functions that have similarly developed over the years. Many readers will have seen historical news footage of searches being conducted by police officers for missing persons, bodies and other evidence. In the past, uniformed officers, wearing their normal day to day uniform, carried out such searches. No training was given and it was very much down to those carrying out these searches and their supervisors as to how this should be done. Now, the SIO will turn to a POLSA (Police Search Advisor) to receive assistance. Such individuals are trained to give advice and direction to the SIO in line with his or her requirements. Searches can involve anything from specific crime scenes or premises to large areas in relation to missing persons, bodies or other forms of evidence.

I do not intend to go into detail about the specific roles and responsibilities, as I will cover this in the next chapter. However, I have used these examples to show the advances made in training and accreditation, towards achieving greater professionalisation. Any officer or member of police staff can expect to be quizzed in court, whilst giving evidence, in order to explore the levels of their qualification. Indeed, as an SIO, I experienced this on many occasions.

Kevin Moore

Therefore, what passed for a murder investigation team in the middle of the last century and what we expect to see now are poles apart. Much of this is undoubtedly due to developments which require a particular skill or expertise, and obviously because those individuals tasked with running such investigations cannot do everything on their own! This has also meant an increase in staffing requirements. As I mentioned in Chapter 1, the fictional portrayal of what constitutes a murder investigation often deviates massively from reality!

Suffice it to say that the professionalisation process involves stand-alone, bespoke training for each role in a murder investigation. This includes the need for individuals to maintain their accreditation through practice 'in the field'. PIP (Professionalising Investigation Programme) is one key element. There also now exists a series of manuals and to assist those involved in homicide investigation. I have already mentioned MIRSAP. There is also the MIM (Murder Investigation Manual) and the SIO's handbook. There are also many registered/accredited experts available through the National Police College to assist SIOs and investigations generally. These cover a whole variety of disciplines including particular areas of forensic science, as well as behavioural and geographical profilers. This is a far cry from what went on many years before!

Let's develop a real case study to demonstrate the difference between times past and now. The case I have chosen is the still-unsolved murder of Margaret Frame which occurred in Brighton in 1978.

Whilst this case was my first experience of a murder investigation, as I had only joined the police a few months previously, my role was a fairly minor one, it has to be said! However, for that reason, I've always been fascinated with the case, partly because it remains undetected to this day.

REAL MURDER INVESTIGATIONS

Margaret Frame

Mrs Frame vanished on 12th October 1978. She was 36 years old. At the time she went missing, she was returning home from a cleaning job at a local school in the Bevendean area of Brighton. She was reported missing by her husband Peter the following day. She had a son, Andrew, then nine years old. The route to her home, in Saunders Hill, Coldean, took her past Stanmer Park.

A police investigation was begun. Ten days later, on Sunday 22nd October 1978, her body was located in a wooded area within Stanmer Park. Her throat had been cut to such an extent that it was felt an attempt had been made to sever her head. It was believed she was attacked from behind, hit on the head and stabbed in the back. Later, it was discovered she had been raped. All her rings had been removed. Potentially, these factors indicated that there may have been an attempt to prevent her identification. From the marks found in the ground, it appears the killing may have taken place a little further away, and that Mrs Frame's body had been dragged to the deposition site where a very shallow grave had been dug. This is what I had been deputed to watch over that long night.

Her body was found following a police search. As already mentioned, searches were then conducted by untrained police officers. I contacted some of those involved, as part of writing this book, and it appears that the body was initially not found. At that time, little significance was placed on a blanket found elsewhere, which was later established to have the deceased's blood on it. Additionally, a garden fork was also seen nearby but not taken possession of. Indeed, it was only the following day, after Mrs Frame had been found, that the blanket and fork were seized when their significance was realised. The body was only found because a young detective constable, named Harry Wood, decided to have a closer look at a particular location. He believed he had seen what appeared to be the tracks of a vehicle, albeit these were never found and may have been a trick of the light. The good news, however, was that it led to the body of the deceased being discovered. It is believed that her body may have been dragged for anything up to 500 yards to where it ultimately lay. Clearly, if a more thorough search had been conducted in the first place, one would have expected the body to have been found earlier. This emphasises my point that police search capability and its professionalisation have increased exponentially over the years.

Fairly early on, Mrs Frame's husband was nominated as a suspect, although at no time has he ever been charged with her killing. He had an alibi for the relevant times, except for 30-45 minutes of the evening that his wife went missing. Some involved on the original investigation believe that too much emphasis was placed on Peter Frame. However, no other suspects were identified. A huge investigation took place following the discovery of Mrs Frame's body. A total of 2500 statements were taken, and more than 5000 homes visited, as part of the investigation but to no avail. The investigation was run from an incident room using the old index card system.

The case was reopened in 2000. However, there were issues with some of the evidence, as exhibits had been stored

REAL MURDER INVESTIGATIONS

in a damp basement area. Things were not as well preserved then as they are now. Indeed, during my time as a senior detective, all murder enquiries, both resolved and unsolved, have been properly documented and preserved. Despite the best efforts of the review in 2000, the case remains unsolved and stays open to this day.

Since 2000, many unsolved cases have been made the subject of a formal review or investigation. These are regularly reviewed, especially in the light of potential developments in forensic science. A good example of this is the so-called *Babes in the Wood* murders, touched on previously, which will be the subject of fuller coverage in a later chapter.

The reason that the Frame case has remained with me right up until now is simply because of my initial involvement in keeping watch of the deposition site. I suppose, as an individual who was later to spend most of his police service as a detective, my curiosity as to who was responsible for the murder developed at that time and will remain with me until such time as the case is solved!

The purpose of this chapter has been to show how things have developed over the years. This ranges from a very basic model of investigation, pulling together many individuals, the majority of whom had little or no formal training, to what we have now, which is a very experienced and highly trained cadre of individuals and teams.

The method of investigation today consists of a very structured approach with embedded systems and processes. There is a model of working which is followed in almost every case. Whilst each case has to be approached on its own merits, the model is sufficiently flexible to allow for adjustment in terms of difficulty. The decision-making of the SIO is formally documented in a decision-making log or policy file. This allows those looking in from the outside to better understand the SIO's thought processes, why key decisions were taken, what was considered in making these and, just as importantly, why other considerations were ruled out.

As mentioned previously, incident rooms are run in line with a nationally recognised approach so that uniformity is achieved. There are formal processes recognised for the purpose of raising actions to be carried out by the members of the investigation in line with the policies and lines of enquiry set by the SIO. More of this will be covered in the next chapter. Suffice it to say at this stage, that every murder investigation recognises the importance of things being undertaken properly and thoroughly, and in line with the levels of accountability expected by families and, of course, the judiciary.

CHAPTER 4

The Reality - The Set Up For A Murder Investigation

When it comes to describing the investigative set up for a murder investigation, it needs to be borne in mind that, like everything in policing, many developments over the years owe themselves to learning from what has gone on before. By this, I mean that, as a result of learning from previous mistakes or through general improvements or system developments, certain levels of resourcing and proper training are required. The most obvious of these are, of course, the roles within the Major Incident Room, many of which are needed to operate the HOLMES system effectively and also to comply with the MIRSAP (Major Incident Room Standardised Administrative Procedures).

However, before I go into depth regarding this and other roles involved in such investigations, it may be helpful if the reader has some understanding of why certain types of investigation command the levels of resourcing that they do. There are now in existence official categories of murder, originally designed by ACPO (Association of Chief Police Officers), now known as the NPCC (National Police Chiefs Council). This categorisation assists those who are responsible for the investigation to understand the recommended staffing levels of each different type of investigation.

The different categories are as follows:

Category A+ - a Category A homicide or other major investigation where public concern and the associated response to media intervention are such that 'normal' staffing levels are not adequate to keep pace with the investigation.

Kevin Moore

Category A – a homicide or other major investigation which is of grave concern or where vulnerable members of the public are at risk; where the identity of the offender(s) is/are not apparent, or the investigation and the securing of evidence requires significant resource allocation.

Category B – a homicide or other major investigation where the identity of the offender(s) is not apparent, the continued risk to the public is low, and the investigation or securing of evidence can be achieved within normal resourcing arrangements.

Category C – a homicide or other major investigation where the identity of the offender(s) is/are apparent from the outset and the investigation and/or securing of evidence can be easily achieved.

The SIO has to decide, very early in the proceedings, whether the circumstances should be categorised as such. This is because these types of investigation can lead to calls for public enquiries, and mistakes can affect the reputation of the police as an organisation.

There is a very good mnemonic as regards murder investigation which should always be at the forefront of every investigator's mind. It's known as the ABC. A – Assume nothing, B – Believe nothing, C- Challenge/check everything.

The Major Incident Room (MIR) is the hub of any murder investigation. Every piece of information and every document must go into and come out of the MIR. The roles within the MIR are: Incident Room Manager, Action Allocator, Receiver, HOLMES indexer(s), Analyst, Typist(s). In summary, actions are raised in line with the investigative policy set by the SIO and current lines of enquiry. These will, of course, be determined by the direction in which the investigation is heading, and depend also upon the documented hypotheses of the SIO. Hypotheses are

REAL MURDER INVESTIGATIONS

essential to the SIO, but these should always cover as wide an area as possible and should be evidence-based, rather than amount to theories. There is a marked difference.

The MIR manager is normally a senior detective of inspector rank, while action allocators and readers are of detective sergeant level, although occasionally detective constables perform the action allocator role. The reader is key, because it is that individual who reads every document and raises the actions for allocation. Therefore, they are seeing every single statement, report or 'other document' submitted into the MIR. With category B and C investigations, the MIR manager can be the reader also and this may be at detective inspector/sergeant level, dependent upon the requirements of the SIO and the classification of the investigation. Documentation submitted into the MIR then passes through the indexer, the analyst and ends with the typists. Every document is typed as HOLMES has a free text search capability as mentioned previously. Dependent on the size and categorisation of the investigation, the detective inspector operating as the incident room manager can also operate as the deputy SIO.

The officers carrying out the 'actions' form the Outside Enquiry Team, normally made up of detective constables and supervised by a detective sergeant.

In the larger investigations, it is important to have available an 'admin officer'. This will normally be an individual with some rank or, if a member of police staff, somebody of a higher grade. This individual will need to be someone who can make things happen in terms of acquiring equipment needed, dealing with administrative processes such as duties, overtime and expenses claims. This role takes away a considerable amount of unnecessary distractions from the SIO.

There are then the specialist support areas required for any investigation. The numbers and levels of management or supervision for these individuals will very much depend on the categorisation of the enquiry. The SIO will sit with these individuals and develop an investigative strategy based on that particular discipline. This is a written document and forms a key part of any investigation, providing an audit trail relating to such decision-making.

The Family Liaison Officer (FLO) is a key position. Many, even within the policing arena, often perceive that this role is simply about liaising with the victim's family and providing the link with the SIO and the investigation itself. Whilst this is a part of the function, the FLO should be an investigator. In some cases, especially those where the victim may have a criminal background, the FLO will potentially receive information, intelligence or evidence which may prove highly significant to the investigation.

The Crime Scene Manager and/or Crime Scene Co-ordinator is a senior crime scene investigator or scenes of crime officer of supervisory or management grade. They will be responsible for operating in line with the SIO's requirements as regards the retrieval of potential evidence from the various identified scenes. This individual will also work with the SIO to determine which exhibits should be submitted to the Forensic Science Service for examination. This is a critical element as forensic costs are notoriously high and therefore some degree of realism as to potential outcome is required. This process may be supported through the use of a Forensic Specialist Advisor who is not a member of the police service.

The House to House manager/supervisor is normally a uniformed officer of sergeant rank, who manages a team of police constables/police community support officers, responsible for speaking to those occupying premises in an area around the murder scene. This area will be defined by the SIO in line with two main objectives. Firstly, to establish whether they witnessed anything relevant to the murder.

REAL MURDER INVESTIGATIONS

Secondly, whether they possess knowledge about the victim or anything else which may assist the investigation. Each person spoken to has a PDF (Personal Descriptive Form) completed about them. This may be accompanied by a separate questionnaire, should the SIO feel that answers given to specific questions may help the investigation. The importance of this function cannot be underestimated but sadly often is. I will, later in the book, highlight a key piece of information that was not picked up during the house to house, which may have made the police suspect the offender Levi Bellfield at a much earlier stage.

The Police Search Advisor (POLSA), and the search team itself, may be required by the SIO to search for a potential body or other evidence, either within premises or outdoors, including a potential murder weapon. The issue of professionalised searching is still a relatively recent development but can be key. There is a real need for the SIO to ensure that the POLSA understands the extent and intrusiveness of the search required, because a failure to do so may result in disappointment and a misunderstanding in expectations, as well as the potential loss of key evidence.

The exhibits and disclosure officers have more recently been recognised as dedicated positions and may be police officers or police staff. In terms of exhibits, it is critical that these are properly secured, packaged and documented, and that any movement is recorded and signed for. This will ensure that the integrity of exhibits is maintained. The disclosure officer is in place to ensure that all material in the form of statements, reports and other documents are properly recorded and preserved. This is to ensure that obligations under the Criminal Procedure and Investigations Act (CPIA) 1996 are met. This is about the need to be able to provide the defence in any trial with evidence that may materially assist their case, or indeed may undermine the prosecution case. Away from murder cases, readers will be familiar with some of the recent criticisms of police in their failure to meet these obligations, specifically in relation to investigations involving rape, leading to cases being lost at court.

An intelligence cell may be required by the SIO in the more complex cases. The size of this in terms of resourcing will very much depend on the lines of enquiry being pursued. There may be a need for authorisations under RIPA (Regulation of Investigatory Powers Act 2000) to be obtained so that the SIO can pursue some of the more sensitive and intrusive types of surveillance. Also, there is often these days a need to examine mobile phone data and other forms of computer hardware and software, which needs authorisations to be in place to ensure that accountability is maintained. There is often a need also for intelligence profiles to be developed and maintained around potential suspects.

An interview strategy will be a key development required by the SIO. This may relate to what are termed significant witnesses as well as suspects. There are now specially trained witness and suspect interviewers to ensure the integrity of such evidence is maintained. The model used is known as PEACE (Planning and Preparation; Engage and Explain; Account, clarification and challenge; Closure; Evaluation). Often, the SIO will employ an Interview Co-ordinator who will be responsible for the development of interview strategies and will monitor interviews held with suspects.

An essential part of any murder investigation is media liaison, which has two main elements. Firstly, murder is, generally speaking, big news. There will be a thirst for knowledge of the incident from the various media outlets, and especially TV, radio and newspapers. Secondly, the SIO may need media assistance in order to get messages or appeals out to the public. Therefore, this is inevitably a two-

REAL MURDER INVESTIGATIONS

way street and as a result, a necessary evil! The SIO will be very busy with other matters involving the investigation. Therefore, it is crucial to have a media-relations professional available, to develop a media strategy to cover all the necessary angles. Over recent years, in the highest profile of cases, a senior police officer has been put in place to remove this burden from the SIO. Good examples of this involved Cambridgeshire Police with the murders of Holly Wells and Jessica Chapman at the hands of Ian Huntley in Soham in 2002. Also, Suffolk Police ensured that this happened in December 2006 when Steven Wright murdered five women in Ipswich. The media invariably wish to speak to a senior police officer rather than a media-relations professional. Therefore, such a tactic suits everybody's purposes.

In the most recent times, it has been necessary, following such high-profile crimes, to consider the development of a 'community impact assessment'. This, as the title suggests, is very much about providing public reassurance to the local community through the local neighbourhood policing teams. Developing a strategy to deal with this falls to the local police divisional commander. Clearly, such matters become of greater importance where, for instance, the murder investigation involves a hate crime, has a racial motive or is likely to affect other vulnerable groups within the community. In the most difficult cases, where there is potential for reputational damage to the police, the SIO will explore the use of an Independent Advisory Group (IAG). In the case of Sussex, this sits at Force level and is made up of individuals, independent of the police service, who may represent different racial or other minority groups, or other key individuals and community groups. They will assist the police by giving a view on how best to communicate issues to minority groups or communities, especially in cases where the police need to gain their co-operation in order to assist or advance the investigation. There may also be a need to ensure that the overall public confidence in the police is maintained.

The role of the Forensic Pathologist is fundamental to any homicide investigation. There is an accredited list of forensic pathologists nationally and regionally. These individuals are pathologists who have undergone considerable additional forensic training and accreditation to be able to fulfil the role. This aspect comes under the jurisdiction of the Home Office. The SIO will work closely with the forensic pathologist allocated to the case through a 'call out' rota. Invariably, the SIO will attend any post-mortem in order to receive at first hand the initial findings regarding cause of death, as well as the retrieval of potentially useful evidence. Liaison with HM Coroner is also a key element and responsibility for the SIO.

It can quickly be seen, therefore, that, unlike some of the fictional depiction of police murder investigations, such matters involve a highly resource-intensive process and procedure. Not all the scientific elements sit under one roof either, as shown in *Silent Witness*! Indeed, the specialists involved in scenes of crime, forensic science and pathology are very much separate entities. If only it were as simple as such programmes suggest!

In order to illustrate how the machinery operates, let's deal with the case of what became known as the *Babes in the Wood* murders, involving the deaths of Nicola Fellows and Karen Hadaway in October 1986. At that time, I was a detective constable serving in the CID in Hastings when, together with a colleague, we were called upon to assist that investigation.

Up until this point in my career, this was by far the biggest case I had been involved in and remained one of the largest, even by the end of my career. It was simply massive!

REAL MURDER INVESTIGATIONS

The media interest, unsurprisingly, was huge. After all, this involved the brutal killing of two nine-year-old little girls. On our arrival at Brighton Police Station on Saturday 11th October 1986, there were large numbers of media vehicles and personnel encamped outside the building. This immediately told me that this was no ordinary murder investigation.

Karen Hadaway *Nicola Fellows*

The girls were originally reported missing by their parents during the evening of Thursday 9th October 1986. They lived with their respective families in Newick Road, Moulsecoomb, Brighton. An intensive search was started by police, assisted by local volunteers. Ironically as it turned out, one of these volunteers was Russell Bishop, aged 20 and known to both families. The bodies of both girls were found a little after 4pm the following day, Friday 10th October, in a copse area within Wild Park opposite where they lived. It was later established that both girls had been raped and strangled.

When Phil Waters, my colleague, and I arrived, we attended a briefing. There must have been around 50 detectives in the room and immediately, one could see that this investigation was out of the realms of most other murder investigations. We were addressed by the SIO,

Kevin Moore

Detective Superintendent Bernie Wells, a highly respected senior detective and very capable of running an investigation of this magnitude. It was apparent from the demeanour of those in attendance just how serious and important this investigation was. You could have heard a pin drop as the briefing started.

Wild Park – Scene of where the bodies of Nicola and Karen were found

The MIR for the investigation was run by a detective inspector, Peter Harvey, and was well staffed. At this time, whilst HOLMES had not yet been introduced, Sussex Police were working from a stand-alone computerised system known as Auto Index. Most forces were operating similarly, and this was the case until the introduction of the first version of HOLMES during the next couple of years. Therefore, the system in terms of how things operated was pretty much as already described.

The investigation was supported by a large house to house enquiry team, the likes of which I had never witnessed before or since. During the investigation, every household on the Moulsecoomb estate was visited, even extending into part of the neighbouring Bevendean community.

Most of the searching had taken place over the previous couple of days by uniformed police officers drawn from across the force. Indeed, considerable resources were drawn

REAL MURDER INVESTIGATIONS

from far and wide so that all disciplines, as they existed at that time, associated with murder investigations, were staffed with sufficient numbers.

Much of the investigation's early stages were focused on tracing the two girls' final movements, attempting to identify potential suspects, and dealing with the retrieval and submission of forensic evidence. Each family was supported by a pair of detectives. At that time, there was no formal recognition of Family Liaison Officers, as we now know them. However, it was critical to obtain evidence and information about those who may have known the girls sufficiently well for them to have gone with the individual responsible for their killings. It was recognised early on that this was most likely to have been the case.

Working days were extremely long and exhausting as the investigation team ploughed on, working through the masses of actions raised by the MIR, taking statements and completing officers' reports. However, despite other lines of enquiry looking at potential perpetrators, both identified and unidentified, it wasn't long before the name of Russell Bishop featured in a major way as the prime suspect. As previously mentioned, he had taken part in the search for the girls during the Friday. Indeed, when the bodies were located by one of the volunteers, Bishop suggested that he had touched the bodies in order to feel for a pulse, although he was later to retract this.

He was well known to both families and had been a frequent visitor to the Fellows' home. He was unable to provide evidence for his movements during the critical times when it was believed the two girls had met their deaths. Indeed, independent witnesses put him close to the scene where the bodies were found.

However, the most crucial piece of evidence revolved around the clothing worn by Bishop on the evening in question. This included a blue 'Pinto' sweatshirt. I still recall

Kevin Moore

the morning briefing where the disclosure was made that Bishop had been wearing such an item. One of the scenes of crime officers, a man called Eddie Redman, left the briefing whilst it was still going on. He had realised the significance of the Pinto sweatshirt and knew that a similar item was among the exhibits found during the search on the Friday.

The sweatshirt had been found by a member of the public and handed into the Moulesecoomb police office, as it was then situated on the main A270 road opposite Moulescoomb Way. It was found on the other side of a fence alongside a footpath which ran along the back of Moulescoomb railway station towards the Hollingdean housing estate where Bishop lived in Stephens Road with his partner, Jenny Johnson. This would have been the most direct route for Bishop to take, bearing in mind the statements already obtained which put Bishop in that locality at the relevant time. The sweatshirt bore some paint which, witnesses were able to say subsequently, came from a car he had been spraying. Indeed, it fell to Phil and me to provide this evidence through obtaining statements from the relevant parties. This included the owner of the car sprayed by Bishop and locating the car itself, which had gone through other pairs of hands subsequently.

This was a major breakthrough in the case. Ultimately, the Forensic Science Service were able to link the sweatshirt to paint samples obtained from the car that Bishop had sprayed. At this time, DNA evidence was not available as it had not yet been discovered, and therefore this evidence regarding the paint was as good as could be achieved at the time. Subsequently, scientific evidence suggested that vegetation present where the bodies were found, was also present on the sweatshirt. There was fibre transference evidence as well, linking the clothing of the dead girls to the sweatshirt. Therefore, a compelling case was being developed against him.

REAL MURDER INVESTIGATIONS

Bishop was arrested but during his interview, denied ownership of the sweatshirt, as well as denying responsibility for the murders of Nicola and Karen. He was subsequently charged with both killings and in December 1987, stood trial at Lewes Crown Court.

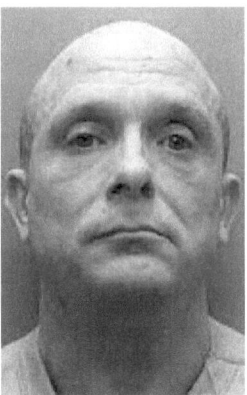

Russell Bishop

This is a broad summary of how Bishop came to be arrested and charged with the murders. Obviously, a tremendous amount of work went on behind the scenes to eliminate other potential suspects, as well as considering other lines of investigation. Phil Waters and I remained with the investigation until just after Bishop was charged.

As people will now be aware, Bishop was found not guilty at that trial. The presentation of the forensic evidence at court was not all that it might have been. Together with this, the defence could demonstrate the potential for cross contamination of key exhibits. This was unfortunately sufficient for the jury to find Bishop not guilty. For all of us involved, the outcome was devastating, as indeed it was, of course, for the families of both dead girls.

However, worse was to follow. In February 1990, a seven-year-old girl was the victim of an attack by Bishop at Devil's Dyke, Hove on the South Downs. Due to the efforts of

Kevin Moore

Detective Inspector Malcolm Bacon and his team, Bishop was arrested and charged with kidnap, indecent assault and attempted murder. On 13th December 1990, he was convicted and sentenced to life imprisonment.

That is where this story might have ended. However, in April 2005, the double jeopardy provisions of the Criminal Justice Act 2003 took effect. This made it possible to prosecute a previously-acquitted person a second time where new and compelling evidence becomes available. In order for a second prosecution to take place, the original not guilty verdict had to be quashed by the Court of Appeal.

During my time as Head of Sussex CID between 2007 and 2009, a case review of this double murder took place. Whilst some headway was made in relation to DNA profiling techniques, these still had limited success. Therefore, there was insufficient new and compelling evidence available to consider a second prosecution.

In 2012, Sussex Police undertook another internal police review which included a fresh look at forensic science opportunities regarding the considerable advances in DNA. In 2013, police were informed that there was DNA potentially linking Russell Bishop to the Pinto sweatshirt. Following this development, scientific examinations continued which served to strengthen the case, as his DNA was found on the arm of one of the girls. This was sufficient for Bishop to be made the subject of a new trial. In 2016, the Director of Public Prosecutions sanctioned the re-interviewing of Bishop which was carried out in May 2016. Bishop continued to deny responsibility for the murders. In December 2017, the Court of Appeal granted the order for the quashing of the original not guilty verdict and authorised Bishop to be tried for a second time.

Bishop's trial began on 15th October 2018, ironically almost exactly 32 years to the day that the two girls were killed. Forensic medicine now provided devastating

REAL MURDER INVESTIGATIONS

evidence of Bishop's guilt, particularly in terms of the samples taken from Karen's left forearm. New tests could now identify DNA, and the resulting findings formed a profile which matched the defendant's. Even though the profile was incomplete, it still proved that it was approximately one billion times more likely that the DNA present was from Bishop, Karen and an unknown person, rather than Karen and two unknowns.

As the proscuting counsel, Brian Altman QC, said in opening, 'How else and when else, did this man's DNA come to be deposited on Karen's exposed left forearm, if not after her top had been removed and during and for the purpose of these sexually motivated killings?'

The new techniques were also used on the Pinto sweatshirt. Results proved scientifically that not only had Bishop been the wearer of the sweatshirt but it was also connected to his home environment and the two girls and therefore their murder. The forensic laboratory also stated that there was 'no possibility' that cross-contamination had occurred.

Significantly, the prosecution also now had the opportunity to rely on his sexually-motivated attempt to kill the seven-year-old girl in 1990, and, as before, leaned strongly on the detailed descriptions he gave of the appearance of Nicola and Karen's bodies, as well as the contradictions in his accounts.

Interestingly, Bishop, in denying responsibility during the trial, attempted to place the blame at the door of Barrie Fellows, Nicola's father. This warrants a mention here because Barrie Fellows was actually arrested and questioned in April 2009, together with others, as a result of new information received around that time. Indeed, Barrie had been questioned about the murders, following Bishop's acquittal in December 1987. The information received in 2009 related to allegations of sexual assault involving his dead daughter, separate to but potentially connected with the murder investigation. Ultimately, following a thorough investigation, no further action was taken against anyone. I was Head of CID at the time and I recall an article appearing in the *Independent* in June 2009, which included an interview with Barrie Fellows. It was highly critical of the police action taken at the time. However, ironically, the fact that such action had been taken assisted in undermining Bishop's claims at the ultimate trial. It was the right course of action at the time as instances involving credible claims require thorough investigation.

Russell Bishop was found guilty of both murders on Monday 10th December 2018, following his trial at the Old Bailey, and sentenced to life imprisonment. Ironically, this was 31 years to the day that Bishop was originally found not guilty of the same crimes.

I have used the Bishop case to highlight the fact that everything that could have been done was indeed done during the original investigation. No stone was left unturned and all the right mechanisms were put in place as part of that original investigation. What was different this time was the critical DNA and other forensic evidence, the retrieval of which was not available during 1986. Additionally, of course, there was available the evidence relating to Bishop's attack of the young girl at Devil's Dyke. Inevitably, it still plays on my mind that another little girl had to suffer at the hands of Bishop before he was removed from the streets and rightly put behind bars. I never had any doubts whatsoever of his guilt, the first time around.

CHAPTER 5
The Role of The Senior Investigating Officer (SIO)

The Senior Investigating Officer (SIO) is very much the figurehead for any major crime investigation. Often, the outcome of any such enquiry will very much depend on the direction set by him or her. Arguably, one of the most significant areas of development in murder investigation has been the professionalisation of the role. As I have previously mentioned, over the years there was little or no formal training for the position. It was very much a case of picking it up as you went along, drawing on the experiences of others. Even in my own early days of murder investigation, there was little formal training provided to any detective at any level.

There is now a formal accreditation process in place known as PIP (Professionalising Investigations Programme). This programme is for all police officers and some police staff at various levels, relating to key aspects required of investigators. The various levels of PIP can be broken down as follows:

Initial Police Learning and Development Programme (IPLDP) – PIP Level 1

Initial Crime Investigators Development Programme (ICIDP) – PIP Level 2

Initial Management of Serious Crime Course (IMSC) – PIP Level 2

Detective Inspectors Development Programme (DIDP) – PIP Level 2

Senior Investigating Officer Development Programme (SIODP) – PIP Level 3

For the SIO, there are clearly defined skills needed, as

well as compliance with the National Occupational Standards (NOS). There are three key areas laid down. Firstly, the SIO is expected to possess investigative ability. Secondly, they should possess and be able to demonstrate management skills. Finally, they should possess and be prepared to maintain their knowledge levels.

SIOs are required to possess an up to date portfolio containing relevant and up to date evidence to show competence to perform at that level. This has served to 'professionalise' the SIO function.

There are also similar programmes designed to ensure operational competence of other roles forming part of the murder investigation team. Over the years, many of the functions, necessary to ensure the smooth running of an investigation, have developed into individual specialisms, the functions of which used to be carried out by available detectives. There is now bespoke training and accreditation for each of these roles.

In the past twenty years, there have been many documents prepared, to assist those involved in the investigation of murder, especially the SIO. The most significant is the Murder Investigation Manual or MIM. This is generally seen as the SIO's bible and a 'must read', as well as being a document that every senior investigator should carry with them at all times as a 'go to' reference document. It is extremely useful for the SIO to be in a position to check that he/she has considered each of the plethora of elements involved in any murder investigation. The document itself is very comprehensive and, whilst not everything contained within it will be relevant on every occasion, it at least assists the SIO to consider whether or not he/she needs a particular element. Subsequent to this, the Senior Investigating Officers Handbook has been published. This is a helpful pocket-sized publication that serves as an extremely useful 'aide memoire' to any SIO involved in homicide

REAL MURDER INVESTIGATIONS

investigation. It explains processes, procedures, and instructions in a relatively simple format, aiming to provide useful help and guidance to those performing the SIO role, whatever their levels of knowledge or experience. Finally, the contents are structured in such a way that information can be accessed easily and quickly.

Does this mean that SIOs are more capable or competent now than previously? In all honesty, I don't think so. Such individuals would have possessed the required skills all those years ago, as well as the necessary breadth of vision and thought. However, there was no requirement or need to demonstrate these in terms of evidencing capability. It was taken as a given that those performing such a role possessed the necessary capabilities. Positive outcomes were deemed to be sufficient proof in their own right. It is certainly the case that nowadays there are a lot more things available to assist the SIO. It needs to be remembered that there is a significant amount of pressure on those performing the role and therefore it is not for everyone.

One of the major developments has been the creation of the Policy or Decision-Making Log. This consists of a record of each and every one of the SIO's policies and decisions and must be comprehensively recorded in the log for audit purposes. Policy books are sequentially numbered in order to maintain integrity over decision-making, and entries are timed and dated and ideally should be contemporaneous. The policy file will contain the investigative strategies as well as tactical decisions and will detail the updated lines of enquiry. These documents, if maintained correctly, are a godsend to SIOs as they demonstrate their thought processes and explain why key decisions were taken and why other potential options were ignored. Crucially, they can be referred to retrospectively in court or any other formal proceedings. Each entry should detail the policy or decision and then below this, the rationale for these. In

Kevin Moore

relevant cases, the SIO should keep a separate Sensitive Policy file. This will incorporate policies and decision-making in relation to sensitive tactics employed during the course of the investigation. The importance of this cannot be overestimated as there are court processes available to prevent the disclosure of the most sensitive intelligence. As an example, this may include source-based or informant-related information where its disclosure may actually put the source at risk.

A good SIO should not only be strong on leadership but also be able to manage, especially in relation to victims' families. They also need to consider the welfare of officers and staff working as part of the investigation team and arguably, most importantly, to ensure the cohesion of that team. Murder investigation relies very much on team effort, a pulling together of minds and ideas. I always used to say that my role as an SIO was similar to that of a conductor of an orchestra. There is therefore very much a balance of skills required by the SIO. Whilst this may appear daunting to some, there is a massive amount of job satisfaction and kudos attached to the role. There is a real opportunity to make a difference and to lead, inspire, motivate and positively influence the outcome of investigations. The role of the SIO is therefore a hugely privileged position.

Two particular cases that I was involved in highlight some of the issues facing an SIO. The first involves the murder of Billie-Jo Jenkins where I performed the role of Deputy SIO. The second involves the killing of the Reverend Ronald Glazebrook where I was the SIO. Hopefully, these cases will demonstrate many of the skills and experience required by SIOs, including some of the pressures they face.

At precisely 3.38pm on Saturday 15th February 1997, a 999 call was received from a man named Siôn Jenkins which was to change many lives forever. Mr Jenkins told the operator,

REAL MURDER INVESTIGATIONS

'My daughter's fallen, or she's got head injuries, there's blood everywhere, she's on the floor.' Death was subsequently confirmed by the attending paramedics.

Billie-Jo Jenkins

I was the 'on call' senior detective that weekend, covering East Sussex. At the time, I was in Eastbourne, attending a Sussex County League football match in my role as Chairman of Eastbourne Town Football Club. Upon being told of the death, I attended the address in Lower Park Road, Hastings, the home of Billie-Jo who lived there with her foster family, coincidentally also named Jenkins. The foster parents, Siôn and Lois Jenkins, had four daughters of their own - Annie, Charlotte (Lottie), Esther and Maya, aged 12, 10, 8 and 7 respectively. Billie-Jo was the eldest at almost 14 years of age. The house was located in a relatively picturesque area of the town, opposite Alexandra Park.

When I arrived, I was met by local detectives who showed me Billie-Jo's body. She was lying at the rear of the house on a patioed area, located in front of a terraced garden. She had suffered terrible head injuries and it was clearly apparent that these had been caused through a severe beating, as opposed to a fall. Indeed, there was nothing to support evidence of a fall. There was a metal tent peg lying nearby which was subsequently determined to have been the murder weapon. It was later established that this belonged to the family. A black plastic bin liner lay next to Billie-Jo and we later discovered that a piece of black plastic had been in one of the dead girl's nostrils. This has never been explained to this day and the reason for it would presumably only be known to the offender.

Home of Billie-Jo is the house on the left in Lower Park Road, Hastings

A post mortem established that Billie-Jo had died as a result of severe head wounds caused by numerous blows, which had crushed her skull.

Initial investigations revealed that, on the day in question, Lois had taken the two youngest girls for a walk along the seafront. Lottie was attending a clarinet lesson and Annie and Billie-Jo were undertaking chores to earn some pocket money. These involved cleaning out a store

REAL MURDER INVESTIGATIONS

shed, which is why the tent pegs were outside, painting the wooden patio doors and cleaning Mr Jenkins's white sports car, which was parked on the road outside the house. Indeed, there was a bucket with water in it on the patio. Access to the rear of the house was via a side passage which had a solid wooden, 6' high gate, halfway along it. It was a bright, sunny day and significantly different to the previous week, which had been the school half term holiday. Evidence suggested that, due to the poor weather during the holiday, things had become fraught within the household, perhaps unsurprisingly with the children being confined. Mr Jenkins was the deputy head teacher at the William Parker Boys School in the town, due to assume the Headteacher's position later that year, following the retirement of the current Head. Lois Jenkins was a social worker.

Billie-Jo was brought up in East London. Both her mother and father had a criminal history and it was decided by the relevant local authority that her mother was unable to cope with her. Therefore, aged nine, she had been placed in foster care with the Jenkins family in Hastings and was attending the local Helenswood School for Girls.

Annie and Billie-Jo decided to swap their chores, so, at the key time, Billie-Jo was painting, and Annie had moved on to cleaning the car. At the critical time, around 3pm, Mr Jenkins drove with Annie to collect Lottie. On returning to the house, Jenkins said to Lottie and Annie that they needed to go to a nearby DIY store to get some white spirit, as Billie-Jo had made some mess with the paint. It was later discovered, during the police examination of the house, that there was already white spirit present in the outside shed. Having arrived at the store, Siôn realised he didn't have his wallet, so they returned home without entering the store. Once back at the house, Lottie discovered Billie-Jo's body. Siôn made the 999 call and sought the help of a nearby neighbour, whilst Lottie and Annie stayed in the 'playroom'. Siôn's actions, from now on, seemed illogical. He did nothing to Billie-Jo in terms of first aid and then went and sat in his car. This, if put together with the earlier aborted trip to the DIY store, suggested his behaviour was somewhat irrational. Crucially, there were around three minutes when Jenkins was at the house alone with Billie-Jo, between returning with Lottie to leaving on the trip to the DIY store. The prosecution case was that the murder took place during this three-minute period. At his trial, the prosecution further claimed that Jenkins had used these movements and actions to construct a false alibi for the critical time. These timings were authenticated during the course of the investigation, through painstaking reruns of the routes taken by Siôn Jenkins.

Great play was subsequently made by the defence of the possibility of another man being present, referred to by the media as 'Scar Face'. During the initial stages of the investigation, witnesses had described a strange-looking man, with a birthmark on his face, who was wandering around the locality. We soon identified and arrested this individual, but he was subsequently eliminated from the investigation through painstaking analytical work. Many of the witness statements made it clear that this man was almost a mile away, across the other side of Alexandra Park, at the critical time. Therefore, he could no longer be considered a suspect. He was subsequently detained under the Mental Health Act. The defence also placed great emphasis on the fact that this man had once been seen curled up with a blue plastic bag up one of his nostrils. This was linked by implication to the piece of black plastic found in Billie-Jo's nose.

A second potential suspect was also identified early on - a nearby neighbour of the Jenkins family. However, he too was quickly eliminated.

REAL MURDER INVESTIGATIONS

Additionally, in the early stages of the investigation, Jenkins referred to instances of prowlers around the outside of the family home. These individuals were never located or identified. The family never reported any of this to the police at the time they are alleged to have occurred. However, these, if correct, occurred during the hours of darkness, not in the middle of the afternoon.

However, the most significant evidence was to come from the clothing worn by Siôn Jenkins. The clothes worn by Jenkins, Annie and Lottie had been recovered by police scenes of crime officers and sent to the Forensic Science Service. On Siôn's clothing, the presence of 158 tiny droplets of blood, invisible to the naked eye, were present. Numerous experiments, conducted by scientists, demonstrated that these droplets could only have come from the wearer using an implement to strike into the pooling of the blood present on Billie-Jo's head. This wearer needed to be in the immediate proximity. The experiments were incredibly detailed. One involved the use of a pig's head. A scientist, dressed in a white forensic coverall and in a white walled area, pooled a quantity of blood on the top of the pig's head. The scientist then used a tent peg to strike the pig's head repeatedly. The outcome was very convincing. The white coverall was covered in minute blood spots similar to those present on the clothing of Jenkins. Additionally, there was identical patterning revealed on the white walls either side of where the scientist was standing, leaving a plain silhouette image in the middle of the blood spotting. The scientist referred to this as originating from an airborne spray of tiny spots of blood. It was argued that this experiment replicated identical circumstances to the fate which befell Billie-Jo. The defence argued that the blood on the clothing worn by Jenkins could have come through Billie-Jo exhaling blood through her airways whilst Jenkins was beside her.

Kevin Moore

During the investigation, Lois Jenkins revealed that Siôn had been responsible for acts of violence against her and the children in the past. She also said he was prone to outbursts of temper. On one occasion, she suffered a perforated ear drum as a result of an attack by him. Lois' evidence was ruled inadmissible as it was deemed to be prejudicial to the defence case. Similarly, suggestions of a previous sexual encounter by Jenkins with a teenage girl were also not heard in court as they were deemed not relevant. However, some of the violence used by Siôn towards the children was witnessed by independent friends of the family and this evidence was ultimately heard in court.

Siôn Jenkins

Additionally, it was established that Jenkins' teaching career had been built on a totally fabricated CV. He had not attended schools that he claimed to have attended, including Gordonstoun, and equally, he had not achieved qualifications, including a degree, that he stated he had. These facts are a matter of record.

These few pages do not, of course, do justice to the painstaking and detailed investigation that led to Siôn Jenkins being charged with Billie-Jo's murder. It took over

REAL MURDER INVESTIGATIONS

two months from the start of the enquiry to the point where he was charged. During this time, Jenkins was arrested twice. He had been released on police bail following his first arrest, pending further investigation. Jenkins' daughters, as well as Lois and family friends, were interviewed in some detail in an effort to tie down incidents and timings, especially those relating to events on the day of the murder. These interviews needed great care on the part of interviewing officers, as it was and is always critical that words are not put into witnesses' mouths, especially when these are children. It was clear that Lois had to wrestle with her conscience initially, before disclosing to officers the details of what had happened to her and the children previously.

Post charge, there is always a considerable amount of work still to do, pending the trial. This involves reacting to CPS requests for the production of additional information and evidence, to further build the prosecution case. Following the appointment of counsel (barristers), there are inevitably further requests. Therefore, in any big case, especially those involving a murder, officers remain dedicated to the investigation in order to ensure that this work is carried out both thoroughly and expeditiously. The number of officers involved depends on the size and magnitude of the case.

Siôn Jenkins was subsequently tried at Lewes Crown Court. On 2nd July 1998, he was found guilty of the murder and sentenced to life imprisonment. Lois Jenkins emigrated to Tasmania with her natural daughters.

In 1999, Jenkins appealed his conviction, but the appeal failed. Five years later, in 2004, following the involvement of the Criminal Cases Review Commission, his conviction was quashed by the Court of Appeal. The basis for this decision was that 'there is evidence, not before the jury, that suggests Mr Jenkins could not have committed the murder'.

Kevin Moore

At the retrial, forensic scientists stated that the microscopic blood spray could conceivably have been released from Billie-Jo's injured airway as Siôn Jenkins moved her. There was therefore a retrial, at the conclusion of which the jury was unable to reach a verdict. In February 2006, following another retrial at the Old Bailey, the jury was once again unable to reach a verdict. A decision was taken by the Crown Prosecution Service that there would not be another trial and therefore a formal not guilty verdict was returned.

On the eve of the final retrial, the prosecution submitted new forensic evidence regarding nine of the blood spots on Siôn Jenkins' clothing which suggested there were fragments of bone contained within them. However, due to the lateness of the submission of this evidence and the fact that further tests were required, the judge ruled that the evidence would not be allowed. He stated: 'All this has come extremely late. It is material that has been served very, very late without any warning that it was coming. I have very much in mind the impact in this exceptional case that a further significant delay will have. Having regard to the extreme lateness of what is now sought, I have decided to refuse.' (As reported by Adrian Shaw in the *Mirror* 10th February 2006)

Interestingly, in 2010, a decision was taken by the Ministry of Justice to refuse a claim for damages of £500,000 made by Siôn Jenkins, despite him spending six years in prison. Readers may find such a decision highly significant.

In England, when a case is undecided, we don't know the details of why, as occurred on this occasion. In Scottish law, a jury can, in addition to a guilty or not guilty verdict, return a decision of 'not proven'. The way in which proceedings were concluded in the case of Billie-Jo was extremely unfortunate and very unsatisfactory for all parties involved

REAL MURDER INVESTIGATIONS

in what was a very sad and tragic case. In a nutshell, the defence's job is to offer alternative explanations for the evidence presented by the prosecution. In this case, the prosecution and defence cases differed in two main material aspects. The first concerned the opportunity for somebody, other than Siôn Jenkins, to have committed the crime. Therefore, inevitably, the sighting of the man with the birthmark on his face, seen in the locality around that time, was something the defence would focus on. I have already stated that, as far as I am concerned, this man was identified, arrested and subsequently eliminated from the investigation. Additionally, I would argue that it should be taken into account that this incident occurred in the middle of a sunny afternoon and Billie-Jo had a radio playing loudly. Arguably, therefore, it poses the question as to whether a stranger would risk taking such an opportunity to commit what was, on the face of it, a completely motiveless and random crime. As previously mentioned, the vast majority of murder victims know their attacker or have some clear association with them.

The second element where the defence case differs to that of the prosecution involves the different emphasis placed on the significance of the blood spotting found on Siôn's clothing. Whilst we, the police/prosecution, stated this had occurred as a result of Jenkins causing the fatal injuries to Billie-Jo, the defence claimed that this happened as a result of her taking her last breaths and were the outcome of blood being exhaled onto Jenkins' clothing via her airways.

What I will say at this point, is that the case was extremely high-profile, with considerable pressure placed upon Jeremy Paine, the SIO, and me as his deputy. The investigation team was highly professional and motivated throughout, despite the contrary claims made by Siôn Jenkins in the media. He stated that, in his opinion, 'the police have been wilfully blind and incompetent'. In

Kevin Moore

response, I would say that no stone was left unturned by the investigation team in an effort to achieve justice for Billie-Jo and her family. The investigation was very well resourced in terms of all the relevant roles being filled. To this day, no other evidence has come to light suggesting a viable alternative suspect.

There was an interesting side issue which arose at an early stage of the investigation. Some of the national media ran stories which were less than complimentary to the town of Hastings. These included issues regarding high crime rates, a previous unsolved drug-related murder involving the death of a man named Bobby Jones, which ironically took place relatively shortly before, as well as the levels of illegal drug use and supply in the town. The local council, together with the police divisional commander, attempted to 'talk up' recent developments in Hastings. This was a distraction, involving local politics, that, as an investigation team, we could well have done without! Having policed Hastings myself, I recognise the challenges it faces, many of which still remain today.

The case impacted on many of us who were involved and will do forever. It remains one of my greatest regrets, at the end of nearly 40 years of policing, that this case was not successfully finalised.

The murder of the Reverend Ronald Glazebrook was a totally different case but is nonetheless interesting from an SIO's perspective. It was similarly high-profile in terms of media interest, due to the background of the case as well as the circumstances of the murder itself. Also, it demonstrates the significant difference between mad and bad as regards the individual involved in the commission of the crime.

On the morning of Saturday, 5th May 2001, I was contacted as the 'on call' Force SIO. It was a May Day Bank Holiday weekend. The request was for me to attend

REAL MURDER INVESTIGATIONS

Hastings in connection with the disappearance of a local retired clergyman, Ronald Victor Glazebrook. An initial examination of the vicar's car boot had revealed traces of human blood and therefore his apparent disappearance was viewed with suspicion. At the time, Rev Glazebrook was 81 years old, still practising occasionally at the local church near his home, a flat in St Leonards on Sea. His daughter, Christine Freeman, who lived in Surrey, had been trying and failing for some time to contact him. She became increasingly concerned, especially when she was informed he not recently attended his church. She subsequently went to her father's home, to be met by a young man named Christopher Hunnisett, aged 17. Hunnisett was unable to give Mrs Freeman a legitimate reason for her father to be missing and therefore she contacted the local police. The initial police investigation had led to me being contacted.

Reverend Ronald Glazebrook

Enquiries had revealed that Hunnisett was lodging with the vicar, with the agreement of his parents who lived in the Hollington area of St Leonards. This was as a result of difficulties Hunnisett's parents were experiencing with their son who had originally met Glazebrook when he became a server/altar boy at Glazebrook's church.

Kevin Moore

Christopher Hunnisett

Bearing in mind the presence of blood in the car boot, a decision was taken to arrest Hunnisett, together with a friend of his named Jason Groves, also 17, on suspicion of the murder of the retired clergyman. While they were detained, enquiries continued which discovered that the missing clergyman owed a yacht named the *Sulis* which was moored at Newhaven. An examination of the boat identified the presence of blood in the cabin area. This was a significant development, along with the fact that traces of blood were similarly located in the bathroom of Glazebrook's flat. All these samples were fast tracked to the Forensic Science laboratory in an effort to identify the owner, as clearly it was looking more and more as if the vicar had indeed been murdered.

Whilst both youths were released on police bail, our enquiries continued which led to the finding of the deceased's head and limbs, buried near a pond in Summerfield Woods, ironically fairly close to Hastings Police Station. This information came to us via some friends of Hunnisett and Groves.

As a result, both men were re-arrested. Faced with the weight of evidence, Groves told the interviewing officers

REAL MURDER INVESTIGATIONS

that Hunnisett had murdered the Rev Glazebrook around 28th April 2001. He and another youth had been told this by Hunnisett himself who said he had drowned him because the vicar had been on the point of evicting him. Groves went on to say that he had assisted Hunnisett with the disposal of the body of the dead man.

At this stage, Hunnisett denied responsibility. However, Groves was able to identify where the rest of Glazebrook's remains were located. According to Groves, Hunnisett had been regularly physically assaulting the old man which had resulted in the deceased wishing to evict him. Groves told us that Hunnisett had drowned Glazebrook in his own bath and that he had then cut up the body. He added that originally an abortive attempt had been made to dispose of the body at sea, using the dead man's yacht, but that subsequently, the head and limbs had been buried in Summerfield Woods where they had by now been found. The torso had been hidden in a bag along what is known as the marsh road, which is the A259 running between Bexhill and Eastbourne. Due to the state of the body, a forensic post mortem could not clearly determine the cause of death, but the pathologist was able to say that death was consistent with drowning. A saw was recovered with the body parts, and a bloodstained axe was found at the flat of the dead man. Another scene, identified by Groves, was on the edge of Friston Forest between Eastbourne and Seaford, where the body had been cut up. Scenes of Crime officers even identified a tree which Groves said had been struck by Hunnisett with the axe.

During his interview, when faced with all this evidence, Hunnisett gave a totally bizarre account involving mythical characters, which made no sense whatsoever. At the time, we believed this was an attempt to develop a defence of insanity. Interestingly, despite being given ample opportunity to suggest that Glazebrook may have been sexually abusing him, neither he nor his solicitor made any such suggestions, either then or at his subsequent trial. Hunnisett was ultimately charged with the murder of Ronald Glazebrook, and Groves with conspiring, together with Hunnisett, to prevent the lawful burial of the body. With the agreement of the Crown Prosecution Service, it was arranged that Groves, who was intending to plead guilty, would be a prosecution witness.

As any reader can imagine, the media interest was intense, even in the initial stages. When it was revealed that the Reverend Glazebrook had been the victim of murder and further, that his body had been cut up and distributed across the East Sussex countryside, it became a media frenzy! Fortunately, after charge, they were very much restricted as to what they could publish until after the trial.

The trial took place in June 2002. Groves, as expected, pleaded guilty and then gave evidence against Hunnisett, who continued to deny the offence. He stated he had awoken on 28th April 2001 to find the vicar drowned in the bath and panicked. However, he was found guilty. As he was 17 years old at the time of the killing, Hunnisett was ordered to be detained at Her Majesty's pleasure. For preventing the lawful burial of the cleric's body, he received a four-year sentence in a Young Offenders Institution, to run concurrently with his sentence for the murder. Groves was separately sentenced to two and a half years in a Young Offenders Institution. Neither youth had any previous convictions.

However, this was to be far from the end of the story. Hunnisett lodged an appeal, successfully claiming he had not been properly defended at the original trial because he had not revealed that he had been the victim of sexual abuse at the hands of Ronald Glazebrook. This was despite the fact that he could have raised the matter at any time during his interviews with police. Also, he could have addressed the

REAL MURDER INVESTIGATIONS

issue with his defence lawyers. The original conviction was quashed by the Court of Appeal and a retrial held in August 2010. During the retrial, Hunnisett claimed he was the victim of sexual abuse and that he was fending off a sexual advance when he struck Glazebrook, and the vicar fell into the bath. At the conclusion of the retrial, Hunnisett was found not guilty of the murder. He was released from custody in September 2010 following the outcome of the retrial.

Unfortunately, there was to be another victim at the hands of Hunnisett, who was to be found guilty of murder once again. In January 2011, just a matter of months after his release, he killed a man named Peter Bick whom he falsely claimed, during subsequent court proceedings, was a paedophile. Bick, it is acknowledged, used social networking sites to meet young men for consensual sex. During the

Peter Bick

night of 10th-11th January, Hunnisett was with Bick at the latter's flat in Bexhill. After sex, Hunnisett brutally smashed Bick's head with five severe hammer blows, before strangling him with a shoelace. Hunnisett then tried to cover the murder up by sending text messages from Bick's phone to his own, falsely stating that the deceased believed he was meeting a 15-year-old boy. This would then lead to the suggestion that Bick was a paedophile, presumably to assist in providing a form of defence for Hunnisett. In summing up at the conclusion of the trial, the judge stated that Hunnisett had appointed himself judge, jury and executioner, believing that sentences received by convicted paedophiles were insufficient. The judge concluded by stating that, from the evidence he had heard, Hunnisett was an extremely dangerous man who may kill again, were he to be released in the foreseeable future. Hunnisett's admitted hatred of paedophiles had become an obsession when he was in prison, allegedly because, when he had come into contact with them, he felt they showed no remorse for their crimes.

This highlights unfortunately one of the frustrations of the judicial system, especially for an SIO. Sadly, the reality is that the process is not necessarily about a search for the truth. It's more about the application and interpretation of the law. Those representing defendants have to apply this, to provide a defence for their clients, regardless of their own personal views as to whether those individuals are guilty or not. Therefore, rightly or wrongly, their job is about doing what they perceive to be right, as regards the law as it applies to their client. Personally, I could never do their job, as my inner beliefs would prevent me defending an individual who, on the weight of evidence, appeared guilty. It is a different matter where there is clear doubt involved. It is not for me to question the way in which Hunnisett's retrial played out in 2010. Suffice it to say, however, that Mr Bick would very likely be alive today if Hunnisett's original murder conviction had not been overturned, leading to his release from custody. It was only a few months after this event that Mr Bick was killed.

What I have attempted to show, in this part of the book, is the critical role played by the SIO. Whilst murder investigation is without doubt a team effort, the success or otherwise of such matters will, to a large extent, rely on the direction set. The SIO is critical in pulling together the

REAL MURDER INVESTIGATIONS

various elements making up the investigation team, in order to produce a positive outcome. Leadership and team building are therefore fundamental skills required of a good SIO. It is simply not enough to just be a great investigator. Whilst he needs to have good investigative skills, the SIO cannot do everything by his or herself. Because there are so many composite elements to an investigation team, each needs to fit together with all the others. The SIO has to ensure that each discipline is very much part of team briefings, by having a representative present so that everyone is kept informed as to progress and what the key lines of enquiry currently are. The SIO should aim to be the glue which bonds everything together.

There is an interesting BBC report related to a typical week in the life of an SIO. Entitled *A week in the life of a London murder detective*", it was written by the BBC's Home Affairs Correspondent, Danny Shaw dated 23rd January 2019, and is available online.

Whilst this particular story relates to a senior Met detective chief inspector, it could be applied to, and is therefore relevant to, every SIO operating throughout the country.

To put what I am about to say into context, in the latter stages when I was performing the SIO role in Sussex, we had four teams of detectives involved in murder and other serious crime investigation e.g. unexplained deaths falling short of murder such as manslaughter, rape, kidnap, serious armed robbery etc. Each team was headed by an SIO. The SIO and their team were 'on call' one week in four, and the SIOs may also have been covering other SIOs' holiday periods. This means they have to be able to respond to the here and now, as well as continuing with existing workloads

At that time, there were 20–25 murders each year in Sussex. Therefore, any SIO and his/her team would be dealing on average with a quarter of these. Some would be

Kevin Moore

'live' ongoing investigations, requiring daily meetings to assess progress and to instigate new lines of enquiry, while others would either have not yet come to trial or be in the actual process of trial.

Some people, even senior police officers not experienced in such matters, believe that the case is finalised when a defendant(s) is charged. Often, the hard work really starts at that point! Such cases continue to require input from the team, right up until their conclusion at court. There will often be meetings with the CPS and junior and senior barristers to prepare for forthcoming trials. Such case preparation is often considerable, usually with tight deadlines.

Apart from the pre-trial work, trials themselves can take several weeks of Crown Court time, during which the court expects a permanent presence of probably two officers to assist the court, as well as the intermittent attendance of the SIO.

Suspicious or unexplained deaths or even potential 'near misses', such as life-threatening stabbings, quite properly take up a considerable amount of time as they need to be dealt with live time. These, initially at least, need to be responded to as if the case involves one of murder/manslaughter in order to ensure that evidential opportunities are not missed or overlooked.

Each team may also have running a 'Cold Case', now made live with new lines of enquiry. Such cases will be discussed more fully later in the book.

There is therefore a considerable 'balancing act' going on each day as priorities are changed and then changed again.

One thing that must be remembered is that the SIO has a management responsibility for his/her team, which includes active involvement in the development of their officers and staff, all of which takes time and has to be fitted in. Therefore, as I have said previously, the role of the SIO is

REAL MURDER INVESTIGATIONS

not for everyone! I can certainly recall times when I have had as many as three ongoing 'live' investigations where the team is still actively seeking a suspect/offender, which is on top of all the other ongoing cases at the different stages.

Occasionally cases involve the potential for reputational damage to the police, and indeed others, if things go wrong. These more sensitive investigations often require the setting up of a 'Gold Group', chaired normally by an ACC (Assistant Chief Constable). These groups are made up of key individuals who oversee the higher level strategic issues outside the investigative process. It requires considerable input from the SIO, as any sensitive elements involved in an investigation can lead to 'political fallout' on occasions.

It needs to be remembered, of course, that SIOs are human and have spouses/partners and families to worry about, as well as their own career development and aspirations! Finally, and often forgotten by some, is the fact that they are also entitled to and should take their days off and holiday periods!

CHAPTER 6
So, Is It A Murder?

One of the questions that I have been regularly asked over the years is, 'Where the circumstances are not clear in terms of how the deceased met their death, how do you manage to decide whether or not the case is one of murder?'

My answer is always the same. Regardless of whether or not the case is an obvious murder, is the death still unexplained or suspicious? If it is, then the same attention to detail, at least in the initial stages, is required until such time as this is no longer the case. This is when it is critical to remember the ABC of murder previously referred to.

One of the most important elements of this involves the Crime Scene Assessment. The SIO and others only get one chance with a crime scene. Therefore, it is critical that no opportunities as regards the securing and gathering of evidence are missed. Once the scene is no longer securely in the hands of the police, it is very likely that evidential opportunities will be missed or lost, if not already gathered. Therefore, the SIO needs to bear this in mind but, at the same time, needs to be bold in terms of decision-making. This may, of course, involve getting independent advice from different experts. However, it should be borne in mind that there are many avenues available to the SIO to assist with their decision-making.

Firstly, a senior scenes of crime officer, known as a crime scene manager, should be called to attend the scene if not already on site. In any event, items located at the scene can still be seized and retained, should they be required in the future. This includes the body, of course. If, in consultation with the crime scene manager, the SIO is still unsure, then they can consider calling a forensic pathologist to the scene.

REAL MURDER INVESTIGATIONS

Before embarking on this, the SIO needs to make contact with the local coroner in order to secure their authority, as any death, whether a clear case of murder or not, comes under the Coroner's jurisdiction. Therefore, they 'own' the body and I have learned to my cost that you forget them at your peril! On one occasion, I took pre-emptive action to call for a forensic pathologist to attend a suspicious death incident but I inadvertently failed to notify the local coroner and to seek consent for this action. Suffice it to say, I never made the same mistake again!

In terms of the scene itself, it is worth bearing in mind the principle introduced by the French medico-pioneer Edmond Locard: 'Every contact leaves a trace.' This means that everyone who enters a crime scene both takes something of the scene with them and leaves something behind - the exchange principle. Investigators need therefore to bear this in mind, both in terms of any suspect, as well as officers and staff attending the scene. Most SIOs are constantly frustrated with the drama documentary and fictional presentation of murder investigations where the SIO enters the scene without having first taken every precaution to prevent contamination. They enter wearing their ordinary everyday clothes, rather than first putting on a sterile forensic suit. As an SIO, I had my own 'go-bag'. In this, I always had a couple of brand new forensic suits of the right size! I have always been a big man and therefore sometimes, there is no XXL suit available at the scene! Out of interest, my bag also had in it an SIO Policy Log, washing and shaving equipment and a change of shirt and underclothes. This, I found, was a must have.

The importance of preserving a crime scene and conducting a comprehensive crime scene assessment cannot be over-emphasised. The evidence that may be available can produce a solid base on which to build or support a case. Similarly, what it tells the SIO can justify a decision as regards subsequently treating the death as not suspicious. Some research previously conducted amongst 32 Met SIOs revealed that the greatest solvability factor that contributed to a successful outcome involved forensic material. The types of information available at a crime scene can assist in determining a *modus operandi*, the linking of people and objects to or from a scene, corroborating or negating witness or suspect accounts, the identification of witnesses or suspects and providing potential lines of enquiry for the SIO to pursue. A huge variety of forensic evidence can come from objects such as vehicles, cigarette ends, clothing, fibres, glass, paint, weapons, tools, as well as bodily fluids such as saliva, blood, hair and semen. Additionally, there may be present finger and/or palm prints, as well as tyre or footwear marks. Virtually anything these days may provide forensic evidence.

The advantage of physical evidence, such as that described here, is that it cannot be affected by faulty memory, prejudice or bad eyesight. However, it is important to remember the need to preserve the integrity of exhibits. This relates to their recovery, preservation, storage and avoidance of potential cross-contamination. Separate crime scenes can be nominated by the SIO, for example, places where a weapon was located or a discarded item of clothing, in addition to the scene containing the body itself.

The crime scene assessment is initially based on the first accounts obtained from witnesses, paramedics and the first police officers attending the scene. It is then completed by either a review of a video recording made of the crime scene or by a physical inspection by the SIO and crime scene manager. I always visited the actual scene myself. This visit could also include the Forensic Pathologist and any other forensic experts. In complex cases, it may be useful to establish a specialist advisory group, consisting of individuals representing the various forensic disciplines.

REAL MURDER INVESTIGATIONS

The important thing for the SIO is to consider logical explanations. In January 1997, I was called out to the body of a man found in a copse at a location known as Shearbarn Holiday Park in Hastings. When I was originally contacted, there was a suggestion that the deceased had possibly had his hands and lower arms removed, in an effort to prevent identification. On attending, I was met by DS John Taylor, an extremely experienced scenes of crime manager. When we looked closely, John showed me that the arms had indeed been severed near the elbow joint. However, on closer inspection, we could see there were marks in the bones of both arms, consistent with them having been chewed by animals such as foxes or badgers. The rest of the scene included empty bottles of alcohol, medication, some lighter fuel and some family photographs. It was clear that the poor man had chosen to end his life and therefore, I was satisfied that there were no longer any suspicious circumstances. As a matter of interest, sadly this man has never been identified.

Probably the most notorious case nationally where the initial assessment of a crime scene went completely wrong is the one which ultimately led to the conviction of Jeremy Bamber. However, it was to be a while before justice prevailed. Jeremy Bamber was the son of Nevill and June Bamber who had adopted him soon after his birth on 13th January 1961. The Bambers were wealthy farmers who lived at White House Farm, near Tolleshurst D'Arcy in Essex. Four years earlier, the Bambers had adopted a daughter, Sheila. Jeremy attended a private boarding school in Norfolk and apparently, felt alienated from his adopted family, as did his sister who went to a separate boarding school. Whilst at school, he was allegedly the victim of a sexual assault and went on to have sexual relationships with both men and women. He left school with no qualifications, much to the upset and anger of his father. He later attended a sixth form college in Colchester and achieved passes in seven O Levels, leaving in 1978.

Jeremy Bamber

Bamber's father financed a trip to Australia and New Zealand, as well as a scuba diving course. While in New Zealand, Bamber broke into a jeweller's and boasted to a friend that he had been involved in smuggling heroin overseas. A cousin suggested he left New Zealand promptly, because friends of his had been involved in an armed robbery. When he returned to the UK, he worked in restaurants and bars, was given a car by his father and lived rent free in a cottage owned by his father in Goldhanger, 3.5 miles from White House Farm. Bamber also owned 8% of the family's caravan park business in Maldon, Essex, which, it was later established, he trashed and robbed.

At 3.30am on 7th August 1985, Bamber contacted the police to report his father had contacted him to say that his adoptive sister, Sheila Caffell, had gone berserk with Nevill Bamber's rifle. When the police attended White House Farm, Sheila was dead on the floor of her parents' bedroom

REAL MURDER INVESTIGATIONS

with the rifle up against her throat. June Bamber was dead in the same room. Sheila's six-year-old twin sons were dead in their beds in another upstairs room, while Nevill was dead in the kitchen downstairs. A total of 25 shots had been fired, mainly at close range. Enquiries revealed that, a few months earlier, Sheila had spent time in a psychiatric hospital where she was treated for schizophrenia. The police believed she was responsible for the carnage until Jeremy Bamber implicated himself to his then girlfriend. It wasn't until this point, when the case had been made the subject of a fuller and more thorough investigation, that the realisation dawned on officers that Jeremy was responsible. Those attending the initial scene had assumed that what had taken place was self-explanatory and took it at face value.

Ultimately, Bamber was charged with the murders. At his trial, evidence was produced to show that Nevill Bamber had not telephoned him, as he had claimed. His father would have been too badly injured to have made a call, if what Bamber had claimed was indeed the case. There was no blood on the kitchen phone and a reasonable assumption would be that Nevill would have phoned the police rather than his son. It was also pointed out that, as a silencer was on the gun when the shots were fired, Sheila's reach was insufficient for her to have been able to hold the gun against her throat and pull the trigger. It was also clear that she would not have been strong enough to have overcome her father, in what evidence suggested was a violent struggle in the kitchen. Finally, Sheila had been shot twice, indicating that suicide was not a feasible explanation.

Bamber was convicted of the murders and sentenced to life imprisonment. He is currently one of 70 prisoners in the UK who is subject to a whole life tariff. Bamber has made many attempts to appeal the findings against him, without success. He has also twice unsuccessfully attempted to secure a share of the family's estate.

Kevin Moore

The significance of this case cannot be overestimated in terms of crime scene assessment. Totally the wrong conclusions were drawn by police initially. The legacy of the case has been that, in all cases of death by shooting, whatever the circumstances, a senior detective MUST attend the scene.

In November 2000, I dealt with a case involving the death of a young man named Andre Clark, who lived in London and had a history of depression. After his family reported him missing, enquiries showed that Andre was seen on the Palace Pier in Brighton and was then believed to have entered the sea. The exact circumstances as to how this had occurred were never fully established. His body was washed up on the shore near Rottingdean, just east of Brighton. This was consistent with the tides at the time. A post mortem examination revealed that Andre had died as a result of drowning and there were no unexplained marks to his body, before death, which may have indicated that he could have been a victim of an assault prior to him entering the sea.

I set up a full investigation with a dedicated team in place, because Andre's death, in terms of his entry into the sea, was unexplained. His family were convinced that, despite his mental health issues, he had potentially been the victim of foul play. The added complication from the point of view of potential reputational damage to Sussex Police was that Andre was black. The Stephen Lawrence case was still very much in the minds of both public and media, as well as the more recent murder of Damilola Taylor. In summary, it was the classic case of, 'Did he fall or was he pushed?' Was it murder, accident or suicide?

Together with the team working for me, I conducted a thorough and detailed investigation, leaving no stone unturned. Andre's final movements were identified right up until the critical time he entered the sea. We located a bed

REAL MURDER INVESTIGATIONS

and breakfast premises fairly close to the Palace Pier, where his belongings were still in his room. CCTV could not assist us any further in terms of his last moments, although he was picked up on this at various times after his arrival in Brighton. It was ascertained that he had travelled to Brighton by train. Many witnesses had seen Andre at various times and statements were obtained from them. The investigation was made the subject of an independent internal review which concluded that all lines of enquiry had been progressed to their fullest. The investigation was wound down as, to all intents and purposes, there was no evidence to show that Andre had been the victim of an unlawful killing. The matter was then passed to HM Coroner for Brighton and Hove.

The inquest into Andre's death was held in the court building at Hove in March 2001. There had been considerable pre-inquest preparation as the family of the deceased had decided to employ a barrister. It needs to be remembered at this point as to what the stated purpose of an inquest is:

> *An inquest is a public judicial inquiry to find the answers to a limited but important set of questions: Who the deceased was; When and where they died; The medical cause of their death; How they came by their death. It is usually the 'how' question that is the main focus of the inquest. The Coroner cannot, in law, deal with any other matters. It is a fact-finding process.*

Unfortunately, families of deceased persons often have an unrealistic expectation of what the inquest will achieve for them. It cannot, in all probability, establish anything different from what has already been found by the investigation. The inquest is not in place to establish guilt on the part of an individual or individuals. It is also not the same as a criminal court - the family or their representative can only ask questions of witnesses; they are not permitted to cross examine them. This means that the Coroner often has to adopt a relatively robust stance, and this was certainly the case on this occasion when it was heard by the redoubtable Mrs Veronica Hamilton-Deeley.

I was extremely grateful that we had conducted a thorough investigation, as when I gave my evidence, I could demonstrate, to the coroner's satisfaction, that every effort possible had been made to try and establish the reasons for Andre Clark's sad death. The coroner returned an Open verdict, which was only to be expected, as there was no clear evidence that Andre had intended to take his own life and, by the same token, there was nothing to show suspicion. It needs to be borne in mind that, given the circumstances, it was highly unlikely that Andre had fallen victim to a completely motiveless act of violence at the hands of total strangers who decided to push him into the sea. I think it can sometimes be the case that families still see suicide as having a level of stigma attached to it and will, perhaps understandably, potentially be very keen to seize upon an alternative explanation.

To further demonstrate the need for open mindedness and the requirement to assume nothing, let's look at the cases of Jane Longhurst and Jessie Earl. Both started off as missing person investigations. Subsequently, in the case of Jane, it was established that she had been the victim of a murder but in the case of Jessie, the original Open verdict of the coroner remains the outcome. Finally, I will also detail a case with which I dealt in 1997 involving a murder, following the victim being originally reported as a missing person.

Whilst I was not the SIO in the case of Jane Longhurst, I was responsible for conducting two independent reviews into the case. The SIO was, in fact, DCI Steve Dennis, a

REAL MURDER INVESTIGATIONS

friend and former colleague of mine. The need to demonstrate complete independence in such matters is critical and I shall later deal with the case of Milly Dowler, in order to cover the review function more fully. However, at this moment, suffice it to say that one of the biggest criticisms of the case involving Stephen Lawrence was reserved for what can only be described as a very superficial attempt to conduct such a review by the Metropolitan Police, fairly early on in the investigation.

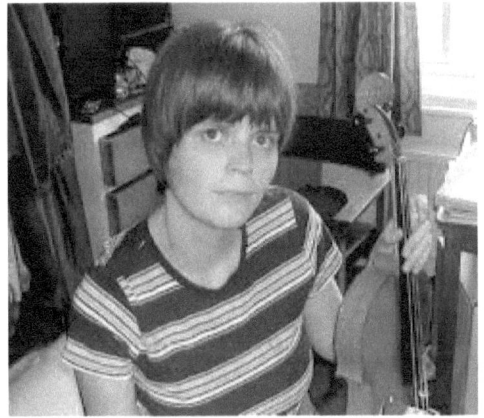

Jane Longhurst

Jane Longhurst was 31 years old at the time of her death around 14th March 2003. She was a special needs teacher and musician, living in Brighton at the time. She was reported missing by her mother and boyfriend. However, very early on, her disappearance was viewed with suspicion. Even in those early stages, the investigation was resourced and undertaken as if it were already a clear murder enquiry. This part of the investigation continued until 19th April 2003 when Jane's partially decomposed body was located, burning in woodland in West Sussex. A post mortem examination revealed she had been strangled.

Suspicion fell on a man named Graham Coutts at a very early stage of the investigation, as he was seen at the start

Kevin Moore

because he was the boyfriend of Jane's best friend. Jane had visited their address and had not been seen by anyone since. Coutts had been arrested and released on police bail. Following the discovery of Jane's body, Coutts was again arrested and during interview, claimed that Jane had died accidentally during consensual, sexually-motivated, erotic asphyxiation. However, there was nothing to suggest that the pair had ever been lovers. Enquiries revealed that following the murder, Coutts had first hidden her body in a shed, then in an empty flat, and finally in a storage centre located in Hollingbury, Brighton. While the body was there, he had visited the location no less than nine times during a three-week period. He had then moved the body to where it was later found. Coutts was subsequently charged with murder.

Graham Coutts

At his trial in early 2004, Coutts admitted to having a fetish and obsession with strangulation. His testimony was confirmed by other witnesses. He had apparently sought psychiatric help with this issue. Coutts had been in possession of large quantities of extreme pornography, which the prosecution argued had been the trigger for his murderous intent and therefore provided a motive. The

REAL MURDER INVESTIGATIONS

defence produced witnesses who claimed that the deceased had previously mentioned a sexual encounter which had included 'some kind of stopping breathing'. However, the prosecution refuted this through evidence provided by both her current and previous boyfriends.

Coutts was convicted of the murder on 3rd February 2004 and sentenced to life imprisonment with a tariff of at least 30 years. This was later reduced on appeal to 26 years. On 19th July 2006, the House of Lords overturned the murder conviction, ruling that the jury in the original trial should have been directed on a possible manslaughter verdict. This, it was argued, would have been appropriate if the jury believed that the death was an accident, caused by Coutts's negligence. The case was referred back to the Court of Appeal and the conviction was quashed and a retrial ordered, which commenced on 11th June 2007. On 4th July 2007, he was again found guilty of murder.

Jessie Earl, a 22-year-old art student at the Eastbourne College of Art and Design, went missing in May 1980. What was originally a missing person enquiry did not quickly turn into a major investigation, even though some officers treated it as such, in view of the unexplained circumstances in which she went missing. Indeed, she had phoned her parents on 14th May, a Wednesday, to say she would be home to see them two days later, on the Friday. She never arrived and was subsequently reported missing to the Eastbourne police.

It was not until March 1989 that Jessie's remains were discovered in bushes near Beachy Head in Eastbourne. Her bra was positioned in such a way that it appeared it had been used to tie her hands. The cause of her death could not be ascertained, due to the body consisting only of skeletal remains. Nevertheless, an investigation, run as if it were murder, was opened at that point. However, there was no evidence to identify a potential suspect. Subsequently, a Coroner's Inquest returned an Open verdict. The police had never actually recorded the case as one of murder at that time.

Jessie Earl

In early 2000, what was known as Operation Silk was reopened as an investigation. However, in the intervening years, paperwork, including key exhibits such as the Jessie's bra, had either gone missing or had been destroyed. This, of course, would never have been the case if the case had been originally recorded as one of murder. Jessie's remains, which had been identified through her dental records, had been retained at Guys Hospital, London within the Pathology Department.

An individual named Mark Williams-Thomas, a former police officer, became involved in the case fairly recently, and connected it to the convicted serial killer, Peter Tobin. I do not intend to go into this further at this point, as I shall cover the case of Tobin later.

Jessie's parents have suggested, in both the national and local media, that the original inquest verdict should be overturned. However, at the moment, there is no likelihood of that happening.

REAL MURDER INVESTIGATIONS

This case shows just how differently cases involving missing people are handled. It also goes to demonstrate that, if not treated as suspicious and a potential murder, then resources are not deployed in enough numbers, and the investigative set up is insufficient. This means that, often, potential evidence and documentation are lost or destroyed. Additionally, opportunities that would have presented themselves early on will have long disappeared, sadly.

Finally, I am going to cover the murder of Wei-Yi Lam, aged 30 years, which occurred in Polegate in East Sussex in May 1997. The deceased lived with her husband, Sze-Hau Tai, at the Thompson Take-Away in Polegate which they ran as a business. The couple had two children, aged 7 and 3, while the deceased's sister also lived at the premises.

Her husband reported her missing to local police on 30th May 1997. As is usual, the missing person report was forwarded for review, after a few days, to the local detective sergeant Keith Lindsay, based at Hailsham Police Station. He was immediately concerned, especially as she was reported to have been wearing only a dressing gown at the time of her disappearance. As a result, Keith viewed the whole matter with suspicion and contacted me. At the time, I was the detective inspector based at Eastbourne, and my area of responsibility included Polegate and Hailsham. The husband was saying that he felt his wife may have gone to see friends and relatives living in London. However, these enquiries had proved fruitless. As a result, I told Keith that he, together with DC Alan Pyle, now sadly deceased, should get the husband in for questioning, although not under arrest at this time.

Due to the thoroughness of the questioning, later that day, 11th June 1997, the husband confessed to having killed his wife, stating he had buried her in their back garden. He was arrested at this point and later in interview, told the officers that, during an argument, he had struck his wife over the head with a large piece of wood, before wrapping her body in a piece of polythene and burying her. Sure enough, the body was found, and the suspect was charged and later convicted of the murder of his wife.

As investigators, we were just starting to think about using forensic archaeologists in cases where bodies have been the subject of burial. The reason for this is that, through careful digging away of the soil, evidence can be identified as to the different makeup of the soil compared with other soil nearby. It wasn't as important in this particular case as the suspect had helpfully shown us exactly where the body was buried. However, in cases where less directed excavation is to take place, clearly such evidence to demonstrate changes in the makeup of the soil could be extremely useful, especially if a body has been moved from one site to another. I was to use the services of the forensic archaeologists subsequently, including in the case of the Rev Glazebrook.

A short funny story emerged during the case. DCI Bill Bunce was my immediate line manager at the time. He came to join me, once the digging for the body had commenced. Bill realised early on that the process was going to take some time! In true Bill tradition, he suggested that he and I adjourn to the nearby pub, known as the Dinkum. We were just finishing our second or third drink when we decided we should check on progress. As soon as we opened the door to leave the pub, the smell told us that the body had indeed been located, despite a distance of at least 100 yards between the pub and the deposition site. It later transpired that the body had been buried for at least six weeks. Having finished off at the scene, we then went to the mortuary in Eastbourne for the purposes of continuity of evidence. However, the forensic pathologist, who had been involved in the dig, decided that the post mortem could wait until the

REAL MURDER INVESTIGATIONS

morning as it was very late. I went home, totally oblivious to how my clothes smelled. On entering our bedroom, my wife, who had been asleep, came to and ordered me out of the house! I had to strip naked in my back garden before re-entering the house to have a shower. Another dry-cleaning bill followed, the next day!

I was, of course, involved in many cases which started off as unexplained deaths. Some are inevitably more memorable than others. One such incident occurred in February 2001. I attended two deaths during one night at a nursing home in Haywards Heath where each of the deceased was face down into the pillows. This was around the time that nationally, there had been cases of nurses involved in the murder of patients. Fortunately, in this particular case, the unusual circumstances of the deaths were purely coincidental. Forensic post mortems conducted on both deceased revealed that their deaths were due to natural causes.

I hope I have demonstrated, through these various case studies, that each case needs to be treated very much on its own merits. Every case is different and if in doubt, the investigator should treat a death scene as suspicious until the contrary is proven, as you only get one opportunity. In terms of crime scene assessment, the SIO, along with the crime scene manager, needs to consider what it is that they see in front of them and always remember the ABC!

CHAPTER 7
Victims And Their Families

Any murder or unlawful killing is a tragedy. Whatever the deceased's background, nobody deserves to die as a result of violence offered by another. Every police officer that I have ever worked with during every homicide investigation has always done their utmost to ensure that justice is done and that the offender is called to account in court.

There are occasions, of course, where the police have made errors in investigations. However, these will not have occurred for any malicious reasons. Similarly, if police officers are involved in investigating a homicide where the victim has a criminal history, that will not influence, one way or the other, how the investigation is conducted, or the levels of effort applied, however serious the criminal history might have been.

Without a doubt, some of the most difficult cases to investigate are those which involve what, on the face of it, amounts to a criminal vendetta. This often means there may be many potential suspects who could bear a grudge or who seemingly have a motive, either to have carried out the killing directly or more likely to have organised it.

Whatever the circumstances, it is critical the SIO and the investigation team do their utmost to gain the confidence of the victim's family. Failure to do so may cause problems, not only in respect of the family's response to the investigation, but also detrimentally in terms of how the media respond. In some cases, certain sections of the media like nothing more than to criticise the police. This may end up detracting from the investigation, as valuable time may be spent attempting to refute allegations made by members of the victim's family or the media, in an attempt to preserve the

REAL MURDER INVESTIGATIONS

police's reputation. I have seen this happen and the unnecessary pressures it can cause. Murder investigations are difficult and challenging enough without having to deal with such issues.

On occasions, the expectations of the family may be unrealistic. It should be remembered that they have lost a loved one and feelings will, in all likelihood, be running high. This is often exacerbated in cases involving families who have spent most of their lives either at best, having an inbuilt suspicion of the police or at worst, are downright hostile towards them. It can be exceedingly difficult for the SIO and their team to win over such families but nonetheless, every attempt possible needs to be made to do so. One critical reason for this is simply that family members may provide the best chance of achieving a successful outcome to the investigation. Who knows better than they the individuals or groups who may have the greatest motive to have been involved in the killing? This is not always the case, however, and on occasions they can inadvertently point the finger in the wrong direction.

In more recent times, therefore, the role of what is known as the Family Liaison Officer (FLO) has become increasingly important. Fictional depiction has not assisted understanding as regards this role. It is often portrayed as involving a uniformed female officer and is very much shown as being about a tea and sympathy approach. Whilst individuals performing the role need to possess good interpersonal skills and an ability to get on with people from all kinds of different backgrounds, their fundamental task is to elicit as much information, intelligence and evidence as they possibly can, in order to assist in progressing the investigation. The FLO is often the eyes and ears of the SIO in terms of the family and its members.

It is essential that the SIO appreciates at all times how difficult and demanding the FLO role is. A good FLO can take away an awful lot of pressure involving day to day contact with the family. In most cases, the FLO is a detective officer and will, in all cases, have attended the necessary training. The FLO becomes the barometer as to how the family is feeling about the investigation. They need to ensure that the SIO is made aware immediately of any developing issues in this regard, as well as potential areas for complaint. They should always maintain a contemporaneous record of conversations, should ensure that the family/police relationship assessment is adhered to, and be present at the regular meetings that should take place between the family and the SIO.

A key function for the FLO is to obtain as much detail about the victim as possible, often referred to as *victimology*. This will, of necessity, include personal and intrusive questions and therefore requires tact and care. It may include searching the victim's room and/or belongings, such as phones and computers, to look for information to assist the investigation. Such information will provide useful lines of enquiry for the SIO to follow. The FLO will also construct what is known as a 'family tree', detailing not only family members but also known associates.

Where it is necessary to Trace/Interview/Eliminate (TIE) a member of the family, this will need careful handling. It may even be necessary to withhold certain information from the FLO, as well as the family, so that they are not placed in a difficult position. A good example would be where highly intrusive surveillance tactics may need to be employed against a family member. Withholding this information will prevent a potential compromise for the FLO. Such decisions need to be properly recorded by the SIO in their sensitive policy log. Indeed, the level of disclosure to the FLO and the family must be controlled in order to prevent the undermining of the prosecution case under CPIA 1996, previously referred to.

REAL MURDER INVESTIGATIONS

As touched on, SIOs should, in managing family expectations, always guard against becoming embroiled in the inevitably emotional pleas from the victim's family. Introducing over-confidence into the family can lead to disappointment and may ultimately impact on organisational reputation. Whilst the SIO should never appear to be unduly pessimistic, they must remain totally honest and realistic about the potential for a successful outcome. In all of my own cases, I was quick to highlight the potential difficulties that I and my team faced, if this was the case. The simple fact is, as explained earlier, some cases are hard to solve. Sometimes, that key piece of evidence never becomes available.

I will now draw on experiences relating to two cases, one in which I was the SIO and the second, where I was involved in its review and then subsequently in the inquest. The first involves the murder of a man with a criminal past; the other, the death of a family man with no criminal history. However, as will be seen, there were in both cases issues between that victim's family and the police.

During the early part of the afternoon of Wednesday, 24th October 2001, Jimmy Millen, aged 27, was gunned down in Tilebarn Road, St Leonards on Sea. He and two associates were at the side of the road, near his home in Carpenter Drive, working on his red Ford Fiesta car. Witnesses saw two men on a black motorcycle ride up the hill towards Millen, before the pillion passenger fired a number of shots at him. Both men on the motor cycle were described as wearing black leathers with black crash helmets and blacked out visors.

Following the shooting, Jimmy Millen managed to crawl to Carpenter Drive, despite bleeding profusely from his wounds. That is where he was found by paramedics who took him to the local Conquest Hospital where he later died.

Kevin Moore

A murder investigation was begun and the SIO initially was John Levett, a good friend and colleague of mine. He remained in charge until December 2001 when he was taken seriously ill. As a result, I was asked to take over the investigation.

Jimmy Millen

It was clear in the discussions I'd had with John, prior to his illness and subsequently when I took over the investigation, that this was no ordinary murder. To all intents and purposes, it appeared to be a form of contract killing, with Millen the specific target. Interestingly, no shots were fired at his two friends.

Clearly, the motorcycle and its two riders were the main focus, but the motorcycle was never traced and there was never either evidence or intelligence to identify the two men involved. That still remains the case to this day.

Jimmy Millen was a well-known career criminal, with a considerable record for offences of violence, drugs and burglary. He and his family had moved to the area from Kirkby in Liverpool, many years previously. A former boxer who now worked as a doorman, he was married to a local woman, Michelle, with whom he had three children.

The investigation revealed he had many potential enemies, albeit that none of these was more particularly at

REAL MURDER INVESTIGATIONS

the forefront as a suspect than any others. John and his team had attempted to draw up a matrix, to better prioritise potential suspects. However, this did not lower the numbers involved or identify the fact that anyone should be accorded a higher priority status than any other.

The other major problem facing us, both initially and later, was the seeming wall of silence which prevailed. The problems we faced can best be summarised from some of the responses received from people living nearby, when house to house enquiries were conducted. Many actually told officers either that whoever killed Millen should be awarded a medal or, alternatively, that even if they knew who the offender(s) was, they would not tell the police! Therefore, the potential for evidence to be forthcoming from any conventional source was dramatically watered down.

Much effort was put into attempting to identify the motorcycle and its two riders and a massive amount of work was undertaken in relation to mobile phones having been potentially used on the lead up to the shooting. At least one witness said that the pillion passenger was using a phone, just before the bike made its way up Tilebarn Road towards Millen, from a turning off the main road. As a result, what is known as a 'cell dump' was triggered. This involves obtaining the details of all phones linked to a mobile phone mast, during a particular time span. However, this is much easier said than done. If a phone is used in any location, it is not necessarily the case that the phone will 'ping' the nearest mast. Indeed, if that particular mast is busy, the phone may 'ping' from another. What we ended up with, as a result, was a massive number of computer printouts relating to several nearby masts. Clearly, from an analytical point of view, priority was given to those phones registering a call to the nearest mast. The idea was then to identify the owners from the numbers. However, as most readers will know, most active criminals use 'burner' phones, bought with a view to disposing of them after they have been used in a particular criminal act. It was a thankless task for those involved but one that had to be undertaken. Suffice it to say that this line of enquiry did not manage to identify a particular suspect.

The FLO involved in the case was DC Paul (Cheesy) Hilton, a very capable detective and the perfect selection for a task such as this one. Ex-military and with many years of policing experience under his belt, Paul could talk to anyone at whatever level. John Levett had set up a regular weekly liaison meeting with the family, following the initial stages of the investigation. I have to say that my meetings with the family proved to be one of the most challenging things that I have ever been involved in, during almost 40 years of policing! To say that the Millen family were universally anti-police, was an understatement. We were, singly and as a group, at various stages referred to as being either corrupt and working with the perpetrators of Jimmy's murder to ensure they escaped justice, or totally and utterly incompetent. This is where the points previously mentioned, regarding the expectations of victims' families, becomes relevant. The Millen family either could not understand or refused to accept that, because of Jimmy's background, people were hardly likely to fall over themselves in coming forward with information or evidence. Despite my very best efforts at trying to explain this, sometimes in fairly brutal and down to earth fashion, it just didn't register.

Clearly, in the early stages, great emphasis had been put on trying to get the family to pass any information to Paul Hilton that may provide potential lines of enquiry or which may identify suspects. The main problem with this approach was that, because of the problems they had had over a period of years with another well-known local criminal family, they became obsessed with them. Each meeting ended up with them going back to members of this particular family, no

REAL MURDER INVESTIGATIONS

matter what I told them in relation to progress. Even when it was pointed out that there simply was no evidence or intelligence to support what they were suggesting, it didn't make the slightest bit of difference to them.

A number of specific elements were looked into, including Jimmy's alleged involvement in drug dealing, as well as specific matters where somebody may have had a positive reason for wishing Jimmy dead. All these were explored as thoroughly as possible, taking into account the fact that evidence barely existed in most cases.

However, the most significant thing reared its head in early January 2002, when the family arranged to come and see me at Hastings Police Station where our incident room was located. Despite John previously and me subsequently constantly emphasising that the family needed to be open with us, as any information might be significant, I could never have anticipated what they would tell me on this particular occasion.

Jason Martin-Smith

Fred and Marian Millen and Jimmy's wife Michelle told me that Jimmy and four others had been involved, the previous August, in the murder of 28-year-old Jason Martin-Smith.

Kevin Moore

Jimmy told Michelle about the murder, the morning after it had happened. She described him as being 'distraught'. She told us that Jimmy had been on his way home from Liverpool when he had a call on his mobile from one of the others involved to say that they had abducted Jason Martin-Smith. After Jimmy had joined up with these other men, he told Michelle that they had killed and dismembered Jason in a lock-up and buried the pieces at different sites in town. Mr Millen thought Jason's head had been burned in a dustbin in a garden already searched by police.

It had taken them nearly three months to reveal this to the investigation team! However, the family very quickly involved the local media, where there was considerable bravado with Fred Millen seeming to 'big up' his son, in terms of his position within the local criminal community, and stating that this is what had led to Jimmy's murder. Fred told reporters he had given police the names of the men he thought were responsible for murdering Jimmy and that, despite this, the police had done nothing, having an inbuilt dislike of his son, and those responsible were still walking the streets. Fred Millen also sent letters to the Chief Constable, the Home Office and the Prime Minister Tony Blair, complaining about our handling of the investigation.

Indeed he had given us the names, but what he failed to tell the media was that we had made arrests, had searched numerous premises and places, including the lock-up, but found insufficient evidence, or indeed any criminal intelligence, to charge anyone.

But the family still refused to believe that Jimmy was shot dead in retaliation for Jason's murder. In my opinion, they failed to appreciate that there may perhaps have been a 'falling out' among Jason's murderers, which led to Jimmy being killed.

This summarises some of the issues we faced. Firstly, there was the overt inference from the family that the police

REAL MURDER INVESTIGATIONS

had failed to act appropriately when given certain information. In addition, they were openly critical of the police. Secondly, they did not consider the murder of Jason Martin-Smith was relevant. Indeed, there is a clear inference that, in their minds, Jimmy's murder was not linked to Jason's, but rather that the motive lay elsewhere. This corresponds with what I referred to previously, regarding their own fixation as to where the blame might lie.

There are two potential elements present. The more obvious involves a case of potential retribution, linked to the murder of Jason Martin-Smith. Additionally, if Michelle Millen is to be believed - that Jimmy was distraught as a result of what had happened - was it possible the others involved could have been concerned that he may make their positions vulnerable and therefore arranged his killing? Of course, this is merely speculation, but nonetheless could provide a reasonable hypothesis, as it is supported by other evidence. It was deeply concerning that the family saw fit to keep this information from us for almost three months!

What this revelation meant practically was that we were potentially dealing with two murders, rather than one. I decided it would be appropriate to link, but to keep separate, the two investigations. Initial enquiries revealed that Jason Martin-Smith had not been seen since the previous August. The normal 'proof of life' enquiries were carried out by us, which inexorably led to the conclusion that Jason Martin-Smith was no longer alive and therefore must have been the victim of murder, as described by the Millen family.

Three men, Frank Torpey, Mark Searle and another man called Steve McNicol were all arrested in early 2002, in relation to Jason's murder. Searle maintained his silence through three interviews. McNicol told police that he thought the others would merely assault Martin-Smith, but not kill him. Millen had, he alleged, told him they 'just wanted to get hold of him'.

Kevin Moore

We approached the CPS with a view to charging Searle, Torpey and McNicol. We believed that if they agreed, this might trigger some new information or evidence coming out, indicating the persons responsible for the murder of Jimmy Millen. However, we didn't have a body and Martin-Smith had been missing for only a few months. Also, it has to be said that, at the time, we were short on evidence and the CPS did not agree to charges being brought.

Both cases were wound down by me towards the end of March 2002.

However, in 2014, Jason's murder was reopened by Sussex Police, and Searle and McNicol re-arrested. Torpey had died in the intervening years. New witnesses came forward who provided evidence supporting the previous evidence gathered. As a result, both men were charged and kept in custody, awaiting their trial. In August 2015, Searle was found guilty of Jason's murder and McNicol not guilty of murder after the prosecution withdrew the charge at the start of the trial, but guilty of conspiracy to kidnap Martin-Smith. Searle was sentenced to life imprisonment with a minimum tariff of 29 years and McNicol received a term of imprisonment of four and a half years.

The whole story turned out to be this. Jason Martin-Smith, Mark Searle, Frank Torpey and Jimmy Millen worked together to burgle a pawn-brokers known as Price Attack, located in Hampshire. The total proceeds from the burglary were estimated to be in the region of £36,000.

Martin-Smith, who had previously met Torpey through a drugs deal, had worked at the store for a short time and stolen a set of keys when he left. At first, he had believed he would only be providing the keys, but when police searched his girlfriend's house, it was clearly apparent that Martin-Smith's role was a more involved one. He then claimed he was threatened to take on a more significant role. He was arrested on 10th July 2001.

REAL MURDER INVESTIGATIONS

At first, he kept some details hidden, but in his second police interview, he identified other members of the burglary gang and told police he only ever received £25 from the burglary which amounted to petrol money.

Almost immediately, Jason feared for his safety, rightly so, as this act ultimately led to his murder. Millen, Torpey and Searle quickly discovered what Jason had told the police. A friend of his revealed that Jason had told him that Jimmy Millen had been threatening him over the burglary as they believed Martin-Smith had 'grassed them up'.

One day during August 2001, Martin-Smith was parked outside an address in Wilmington Road, Hastings, visiting a friend. He was in possession of a gun and was also carrying a chisel in his trousers, afraid he might be attacked. Indeed, he had told a friend that he had the weapons to protect himself against Jimmy Millen specifically.

Witnesses at the trial in 2015 heard that Steve McNicol made a phone-call to say, 'He's outside'. Another witness heard him say, 'You'd better get here quick, he's going.' Mark Searle was then seen running towards Jason, while the court heard evidence that Jimmy had shouted 'Jason!' Martin-Smith was then set upon, outside the Wilmington Road address, by Mark Searle and Jimmy Millen, after they had received the phone call from Steve McNichol. Jason was beaten up and forced into the front passenger seat of a black car that pulled up alongside.

The following day, two men saw Searle, Millen and a third man with an axe, in a lock-up in Battle Road, Hastings. A witness said that, when he went into the lock-up, he heard the sound of an axe hitting concrete and saw what he believed to be a torso on the floor. Another witness said Searle appeared to have blood on his legs. Millen later told the witness's brother that Martin-Smith had been shot six times, one of which was possibly in the eye, and then strangled with fridge wire.

Kevin Moore

Two months after the attack on Martin-Smith, Millen was shot as he worked on his car in Tile Barn Road, Hastings, on 24th October 2001. His killing has yet to be solved.

Steve McNicol   *Mark Searle*

A somewhat funny story emerged after the Millen family passed us the information about the murder of Jason Martin-Smith. They believed that, because they had provided this evidence, their lives may be in danger. As a result, they agreed to put themselves forward for protection under the witness protection scheme. The necessary procedures were put in place and ultimately, they were rehoused in the north of the country. Under the terms of the scheme, attempts are made to match like for like, in terms of the lifestyle of those entering the scheme.

After a very short time, the Millens decided, of their own volition and without telling their handling officers, to abandon the scheme and return to their homes in St Leonards. Imagine my face when, a day or so later, I received a call from a reporter at the local *Hastings and St Leonards Observer* who stated that the Millens were very upset that the scheme would not, amongst other criticisms, pay for the children to have pony riding lessons. I asked the reporter whether they had pony riding lessons whilst they lived locally. When she stated she didn't know, I said that

REAL MURDER INVESTIGATIONS

they didn't and therefore, why should they expect the tax payer to fund such events for them! Honestly, it just goes to prove you cannot please some people!

In all seriousness, however, despite all the criticisms levelled at us on the investigation team, it remains a regret of mine that the murder of Jimmy Millen remains unsolved. No SIO likes to have such matters outstanding. However, some cases are just very hard to solve and this proved to be one of the most difficult cases that I encountered. The team did all we could to obtain justice for Jimmy, despite what his family might think. The case was made the subject of two independent, albeit internal, reviews, with the second of these taking place just before I wound down the investigation. The reviews were conducted by an experienced SIO, Dave Gaylor, who did not identify any new lines of enquiry or any investigative opportunities that had been missed.

Sadly, it is likely that the case will remain unsolved, unless loyalties within the relevant criminal fraternity change, and someone decides to come forward with information that might lead to the arrest and conviction of Jimmy's killer. A reward of £10,000 is still available to anyone providing such information leading to an arrest and conviction.

The controversial case involving the death of Jay Abatan followed an incident that occurred on 24th January 1999. Before I go into detail, I wish to point out a couple of things. Firstly, any unexplained death or one resulting from an act of violence is tragic as, more often than not, it was totally avoidable. Secondly, the views that I express here are in no way designed to offend but are honestly held, based on what I know of the case, as well as my experience over many years of investigating unlawful deaths and murders. My views may not be shared by others and that is their right, the same as it is my right to express my own. I am using the case to demonstrate key points relevant to this book. If an investigation does not go well in the early stages, then often it will fail subsequently. This is mainly because key evidence, which may have been available early on, is not available any longer. Secondly, should circumstances escalate subsequently as regards any investigation, then inevitably questions will be asked, and honesty should prevail in terms of the police accounting for any issues identified. The benefit of hindsight is a wonderful thing and it is easy to point out, after an event has occurred, that things could and should have been dealt with better. It is the case, unfortunately, that there are many incidents, when assaults take place, especially on a Friday or Saturday night, particularly in major towns and cities across the country. Often, these are linked to the consumption of alcohol, tempers become frayed and fights ensue. Undoubtedly, the incident leading to Jay's death was initially treated as another such event. It was not until Jay's condition deteriorated in hospital that things escalated in terms of the police investigation, although this was flawed. The next point is that, once the police lose the confidence of a victim's family, it is rarely, if ever, regained. Indeed, one family member has, quite ludicrously, suggested that there was in existence some form of relationship or friendship between a serving police officer and the suspects. This had, it was suggested, affected the outcome of the investigation. There was never any evidence to suggest that this was the case and I find the suggestion totally disrespectful. The bottom line, however, when the relationship between the police and the family breaks down, is that cooperation is often withdrawn. The result is that the investigation becomes more about the family's lack of confidence in the police than it does about the investigation achieving a positive outcome. It also means that, potentially at least, the family may interpret

REAL MURDER INVESTIGATIONS

subsequent police activity with suspicion and as something designed to act against their interests. This is especially the case as regards media interest, it has to be said. These are the points I wish the reader to bear in mind as they read on.

In summary, Jay Abatan, aged 42, was enjoying a night out at the Ocean Rooms in Brighton with his brother Michael and a friend, Lloyd Jeffers, on 24th January 1999. Jay lived in Eastbourne, East Sussex with his partner, Tanya Haynes, and two children. He was a decent man, with nothing to suggest that he was anything other than that.

Jay Abatan

The incident leading to Jay's death occurred as the three were leaving the Ocean Rooms. They had ordered a taxi to take them home. When they were outside, a dispute took place between their group and another which included two local men, Graham Curtis and Peter Bell. The Abatan group thought that the other group had taken their taxi. It is believed that Jay was punched twice in the face, with such force that he fell to the ground, striking his head on the pavement. He was taken to hospital but sadly died five days later on 29th January 1999.

Well before Jay's condition worsened, the case had been properly escalated to the local CID for investigation and was overseen by a detective inspector and effectively run by a

Kevin Moore

The Ocean Rooms, Brighton

detective sergeant and members of his team. Following Jay's death, a centrally based detective superintendent was consulted, but a decision was taken that the case would remain with the local division to investigate. At this time, Sussex Police, as was the case with many other provincial forces, did not have a dedicated major crime investigation team. What was in place was fairly ad-hoc in terms of drawing together an investigation team, as has been already described in chapter two. It was not unusual, therefore, for such a case to remain with division. Indeed, as a locally based detective inspector previously, I had led relatively straightforward cases of murder and manslaughter myself. What should arguably have occurred, however, is that senior detective oversight should have been more apparent. This would hopefully have led to the investigation being run properly, in terms of procedure, and crucially, that it was resourced appropriately.

In terms of procedure, it was not the type of case that would have warranted the use of a full HOLMES Incident Room. However, the principle as to how such investigations are run should still have been applied, and the correct paper documentation used. Sadly, this was not the case and therefore when the case was made the subject of a review, it quite rightly attracted criticism. Having said that, I had

REAL MURDER INVESTIGATIONS

previously run such cases without using this level of formality. I guess, therefore, it is a classic case of there but for the Grace of God, go I!

However, what should not be lost sight of is the fact that both Peter Bell and Graham Curtis were arrested within a short time of the incident. Indeed, after Jay's death and following consultation with the Crown Prosecution Service, the men were charged with manslaughter. However, the charge of manslaughter was subsequently withdrawn and substituted with charges of affray and assault occasioning actual bodily harm. In May 2000, both men were subsequently found not guilty of these charges. I do not intend to argue the legal niceties of such decision-making or the eventual outcome. Suffice it to say, that the conclusion was clearly unsatisfactory from all perspectives but especially for Jay's family.

As a result of complaints made by the family during 1999, Essex Police were called in by Sussex Police to conduct a review of the investigation. It would be correct to say that the findings were highly critical with 57 observations made. However, the majority of the criticism related to the fact that the investigation had not been run in accordance with MIRSAP, and the correct documentation utilised for this purpose.

Following, the findings of the report and the completion of the judicial proceedings, Sussex Police launched a second investigation towards the end of 2000. This new enquiry was to cost around £2 million. For Ken Probert, then detective superintendent, and Martin Cheeseman, then a detective chief inspector, who ran the second investigation, it was a no-win situation. Ultimately, I guess the process was seen by some as arguably more important than the outcome, as there was little likelihood of finding anything new that was not available at the time of the first enquiry. An internal review of the second investigation was commissioned which

Kevin Moore

was split into three sections. I was chosen to look at one particular element involving the lines of enquiry followed as part of the investigation. From what I can recall, everything that could possibly have been done was done. The SIO had declared the case as one involving a racially motivated attack. It is still my opinion that there was absolutely no evidence whatsoever to substantiate that the racial origins of Jay, his brother or friend had any part to play in what took place. There were no words uttered by those responsible for assaulting Jay to suggest that this was the case. However, it would be fair to say that this led to a media frenzy in some quarters, with some even linking it to the Stephen Lawrence case, implying that Sussex Police had been, potentially at least, guilty of institutionalised racism, as defined by the Macpherson enquiry. Yes, in terms of the strict definition of a racially motivated incident, the criteria were met. However, it needs to be borne in mind that, under that definition, 'any person' can claim an incident to be so. Would the media have been as interested in the case or reported 'police blunders' if the deceased had been white? I will quite deliberately leave that question to be considered by the readers of this book.

The whole emphasis had now shifted to one of demonstrating within the media the view that Sussex Police had failed Jay's family because of his race, rather than through a failing in their duty to investigate the case correctly. However, in attempting to apply some rational thinking, my question is this: 'Would it have made any difference to the ultimate outcome of the case if investigative procedures had been followed to the letter and the correct paperwork used?' This is, of course, what is at the heart of the argument. I am not sure it would have made a significant difference, in terms of securing enough evidence to gain a guilty verdict. Certainly, the second investigation did not move the investigation forward in any

REAL MURDER INVESTIGATIONS

significant way. Indeed, it had the benefit of huge numbers of resources and so could look into absolutely every possible aspect. However, it did not achieve what the family were hoping for.

The word 'murder' has constantly and consistently been used by the media to describe what happened to Jay. Even to the most optimistic observer, this case did not amount to a murder. Manslaughter, maybe. However, there is a total lack of evidence to justify a charge of murder. This is why, even at an early stage, the CPS charged an offence of manslaughter. I recall dealing with a case when I was a detective inspector at Eastbourne in April 1993. This involved two rough sleepers who, whilst under the influence of drink, became involved in a fight with each other. This resulted in one of the men being struck and falling to the ground. In doing so, he struck his head on a pavement. He was found dead a few days later, with the cause of death being attributed to the blow to the back of his head, caused through the fall after having been struck. This is an almost identical set of circumstances to that involving the death of Jay Abatan. We were advised by the CPS to charge an offence of manslaughter in that particular case. However, the case was dropped, as there was too little evidence to link the act of the perpetrator to the ultimate death. Similarly, with the case of Jay Abatan, it is by no means certain that a charge of manslaughter would succeed in court, as indeed it hadn't succeeded in 2000. Undoubtedly, there was a lack of evidence available to say exactly who had thrown the punch which caused Jay to fall to the ground and strike his head.

My other involvement in this case arose during my time as Head of Sussex CID. I was in liaison with HM Coroner for Brighton, Veronica Hamilton-Deeley, as regards holding the inquest into Jay's death. Due to the various enquiries and proceedings, the inquest had still not been held by 2008/2009. A preliminary inquest was held on the lead up to my retirement, which occurred in September 2009. It was clear at that point that this was going to be no ordinary inquest. Indeed, it was to run over a period of weeks. I had left by the time the inquest concluded in October 2010.

In returning a verdict that Jay Abatan was unlawfully killed, Mrs Hamilton-Deeley stated that whilst he was the victim of an 'unprovoked attack', she also said that 'the assault *inadvertently* (my emphasis) resulted in his death'. Therefore, whilst a Coroner's verdict has no bearing on criminal court procedures, there is little doubt that there is no evidence to suggest that the attack on Jay amounted to a case of murder. Indeed, in considering the earlier definitions in this book, the case at best involves one of involuntary manslaughter and may even have been considered to be accidental. The Coroner also went on to say that the attack on Jay was 'entirely unprovoked and entirely unexplained'. No suggestion here, then, that the attack was racially motivated.

Graham Curtis, one of the two men originally charged with Jay's manslaughter, committed suicide in June 2003. It was never clear as to whether the Abatan case was a contributory factor to this event.

The officers involved in the original investigation were the subject of an investigation by the then PCA (Police Complaints Authority), subsequently known as the IPCC (Independent Police Complaints Commission) and now named the IOPC (Independent Office for Police Conduct). This investigation was undertaken by Avon and Somerset Police, led by the then Deputy Chief Constable of that force, Ken Jones. Ironically, very shortly after this, he was appointed Chief Constable of Sussex Police and later knighted. The detective superintendent involved was fined thirteen days pay at the misconduct tribunal. The detective inspector and detective sergeant, who, by this time, was also a detective inspector, received admonishments. The overall

REAL MURDER INVESTIGATIONS

finding of the inquiry was that the original investigation had suffered from disorganisation and a lack of resources. The report of Avon and Somerset was highly critical of the way in which the investigation had been run. Since this time, Sussex Police have consistently apologised for what occurred and have made it clear that, should fresh evidence come to light, then this will be fully investigated.

In dealing with this case, I have attempted to be dispassionate in my views and therefore to provide a balanced view on the circumstances. It is very clear that the way in which the investigation was run was procedurally flawed. However, it needs to be remembered that two suspects were in custody within 24 hours of the assault taking place. As highlighted previously, this type of assault is far from unusual, unfortunately. What probably didn't happen was somebody having the foresight to appreciate what would happen if things did not progress in a positive manner, in terms of outcome. This would undoubtedly have triggered a lot more activity than it ultimately did. However, hindsight is a wonderful thing.

What I have also tried to achieve is an understanding as to the ramifications if things go wrong during the course of such investigations. In that regard, this is an excellent case study. It demonstrates how a victim's family can quickly be 'lost' and organisational reputation damaged. It also serves to show how everyone involved, and in particular the media, can become distracted from the facts and potentially distort what appears before them. The saddest thing arising from all of this, in this particular case, is that the full circumstances of Jay Abatan's death are still not known, even though 20 years have elapsed since his death. It is very likely they never will. It is very unfortunate that the family have been unable to achieve some form of closure. Even as I am writing this book, a candlelit vigil is once again being held outside Brighton Police Station by Jay's family.

CHAPTER 8
Murder Reviews

In the summer of 2002, I was promoted to detective superintendent by the then Chief Constable Ken Jones. My task was to set up a process and structure to undertake major crime, and in particular, murder reviews. Whilst my role was expanded to include other things subsequently, that was my initial direction.

In the past, various attempts had been made by forces to undertake reviews into homicide investigations. These were usually reserved for the most serious or high profile cases, or if things were thought to have gone wrong. This was highlighted in the previous chapter when Essex Police were called in to review the enquiry relating to the death of Jay Abatan. Similarly, the Metropolitan Police were tasked with reviewing the murder of Richard Watson in East Grinstead, which occurred in December 1996. The report provided on that occasion was once again highly critical of Sussex Police.

The prevailing view at the time bore a somewhat negative connotation as such reviews were inevitably commissioned when it was thought that things had gone wrong. However, as will be seen, the purpose of a review is actually to support the investigation process but at the same time be critical, if necessary, of the actions taken or not taken. Caution needs to be applied here because there is a balance to be achieved. As previously touched on, one of the most severe criticisms of the Stephen Lawrence investigation involved a review which took place in the relatively early stages. This review was largely superficial and made no critical comments about the actions taken at that point. We now know, of course, that consideration should have been given at an early stage to arresting identified suspects, two of whom were belatedly

REAL MURDER INVESTIGATIONS

convicted of Stephen's murder. The report that was prepared following the review was hugely supportive of the way in which the investigation was moving at that time. Clearly, this shouldn't have been the case and was wholly inaccurate in that regard.

As a result, all reviews should be as independent as can be achieved, bearing in mind the size of the majority of provincial forces, as most reviews will be conducted internally. It is unrealistic to outsource a review for each and every murder that takes place each year within the UK. Dependent on the type of review and its terms of reference, some can be extremely time-consuming and resource-intensive in terms of staffing.

Around the time of my appointment, the importance of carrying out reviews had started to be discussed at a national level. However, most forces were still trying to understand what this might look like, longer term. Therefore, few forces had advanced very far in this regard. Taking into account the fact that it was in 1998 that the then ACPO, (Association of Chief Police Officers, now NPCC – National Police Chiefs Council), had issued revised guidance for conducting major crime reviews, things were moving pretty slowly! Additionally, very few forces had any dedicated resources assigned to this function. When commissioned, these were largely undertaken by one of the force's existing SIOs. As I was to identify, Sussex was actually one of the first to dedicate staff to the function.

The Murder Investigation Manual lays out the objectives and benefits of reviews. In the main, a review should ensure that an investigation conforms to nationally approved standards; it is thorough; it has been conducted with integrity and objectivity; no investigative opportunities have been overlooked and any good practice is identified. There is implicit within this an acceptance that the SIO and reviewing officer should ensure there is present a spirit of co-operation. Also, that the review should be seen as assistance and support to the ongoing investigation, rather than a threat.

Reviews should actually be considered not only for currently ongoing and unsolved crimes but also for solved offences. However, in reality, very few of the latter type are undertaken, due to time pressures and resourcing. The review may support the current direction of the investigation. Equally, the process may reveal aspects of the investigation which should be pursued or modified. Any review should be seen as an opportunity to improve working practices by identifying lessons learned or areas of good practice.

A distinction needs to be made between a formal review process and day to day senior management supervision of the investigation, as there is a clear difference. It should be for Chief Officers to ultimately commission reviews and determine or sanction its terms of reference. Also, it is their function to appoint a review officer where no dedicated role exists. The timing of reviews is critical. Consideration should be given to conducting one at seven days if the case has not been solved, or a maximum of twenty-eight days. In Sussex, it was proposed by me and subsequently agreed, that a brief review would be conducted after 24 hours, in addition to the others mentioned. This was because we considered that time period to be crucial insofar as, if mistakes are going to be made, often they occur in the very early stages. This has its origins in the so called 'Golden Hour'.

If an investigation is running for a long period of time, then the review should be an ongoing process, albeit that this may not require the completion of a formal report after the initial document is published. Certainly, a full review should be carried out before any undetected case is 'closed down'. There is also a need to consider a regular review of

REAL MURDER INVESTIGATIONS

undetected murders, including so called long term 'cold or unsolved/unresolved cases'. In this context, 'undetected' is defined as one where a full investigation has taken place, but the case has been closed because all possible lines of investigation have been completed. Despite this, the case has not progressed far enough for criminal charges to have been brought. The advances in forensic science techniques, as previously discussed in the *Babes in the Wood* case, mean that every effort should be made to consider the potential to solve an outstanding case in the future. Guidance determines that all outstanding cases should be the subject of a review at least every two years.

The guidance also lays down that the reviewing officer should possess a career profile which includes recent and relevant investigative experience. This ensures that the SIO has confidence in matters then raised with him/her. When I was initially appointed, Ken Jones told me that the reason I was getting the job was because, in his opinion, I was the most experienced and best SIO. You cannot ask for a better reference than that! The need for this is highlighted in terms of the relationship between the SIO and the review officer. A key element leading up to the review is for the review officer to receive a full briefing from the SIO. It may be at this stage that the reviewer passes any immediate observations to the SIO. Therefore, the need for the two to be able to work together, and for the SIO to have confidence in the reviewing officer, is critical.

It is likely to be the case that only the most high-profile cases will attract the need for a review by an outside force.

In the larger and more complex cases, consideration should be given to supporting the review officer with individuals who can review different aspects of the investigation, such as a HOLMES computer operator, family liaison and scenes of crime. I will deal with this again when I move on to my case study of the murder of Milly Dowler.

Kevin Moore

The terms of reference need to be agreed between the relevant chief officer and the review officer and recorded. These should then be agreed with the SIO. These need to be relevant, focused and aimed at establishing the effectiveness of the investigation, especially in relation to scene management, forensic strategy and the major lines of enquiry.

The review's primary objective is to assist the SIO to solve the crime. Therefore, operational matters should take priority over administrative issues. The SIO and their senior management team should be made aware of any problems identified, or anything else requiring immediate attention. Regular meetings during the review can assist with this.

On completion of the review, the reviewing officer will prepare a report and submit it to the chief officer who commissioned the review. Before the report is submitted, the SIO should be allowed to read it, to check for fact and emphasis, and then asked for any initial responses they may wish to make. These observations are then forwarded to the chief officer along with the report.

The chief officer should then consider whether to adopt the findings of the review, and in particular, the recommendations, lessons learned or organisational issues and good practice.

In line with national guidance, Sussex developed a review panel, chaired by the relevant ACC (Crime) which was held monthly to consider recommendations arising from reviews. These meetings also included reviews relating to uniformed operations, which concerned matters involving public order demonstrations or firearms operations.

What quickly became apparent during the time that I was setting up a system for Sussex Police, was that other forces wished to come and see what we were doing, with a view to 'borrowing' many of the concepts. As a result, I suddenly became very popular! I had no issue with this at all as I have

REAL MURDER INVESTIGATIONS

always believed that there is no need to reinvent what already exists.

The murder of Milly Dowler highlighted how a review process should work. There were learning points for all of us during the course of this.

Many readers will have seen the TV drama documentary entitled *Manhunt,* shown on ITV in January 2019. This programme covered elements of the Milly Dowler investigation, but more widely the enquiry led by DCI Colin Sutton which resulted in the arrest and conviction of Levi Bellfield for a series of murders of young women and girls. Colin Sutton was played by Martin Clunes. The three-part production was well done overall, probably because Colin was directly involved in making the programme.

Bellfield was convicted on 25th February 2008 of the murders of Marsha McDonnell and Amelie Delagrange, and the attempted murder of Kate Sheddy, and was sentenced to life imprisonment. However, it was not until 23rd June 2011 that Bellfield was finally convicted of the murder of Milly Dowler. The judge recommended that Bellfield never be released.

The programme portrayed the fact that Colin Sutton received no co-operation when he tried to convince Surrey Police of the potential links between his London Met investigation and their enquiry into Milly's murder. As I have said, Colin was integral to the making of the programme and therefore, as a viewer, I am inclined to believe that this was indeed the case. If we accept that it was, then this does nothing to increase the confidence of the public as regards reassurances that different police forces are prepared to work together, when a potentially linked series of offences as serious as murder is identified.

Thankfully, this is not my personal experience. In late 2001, I completed a course for SIOs and chief officers, then entitled the 'Management of Linked Series and Serious Crime Course'. The course was designed to ensure that, where a linked series involving serious crime, e.g. murder, rape and armed robbery, took place, there is a need to set up a particular investigative structure. In short, this involves each affected force setting up an incident room and a team as usual to investigate their own offence(s). There is then a lead force identified and a chief officer at ACC (Assistant Chief Constable) level identified whose force, whilst also investigating their own case(s), will run what is known as the 'Central Index'. That ACC will oversee the whole investigation in its entirety and is known as the OIOC (Officer in Overall Command). The Central Index is an incident room linking together all the separate incident rooms. Whilst this would probably not have been necessary in the case being discussed, it does serve to demonstrate that forces do need to operate in a formalised way, as regards linked investigations. However, unfortunately, this does not stop the odd occasions where personalities come into play, preventing the development of a professional working relationship. Sadly, this only undermines the overall aims and objectives of any investigation, which is to achieve a positive outcome.

Readers will recall that, earlier in the book, I referred to the fact that serial killings are very fortunately quite rare. Indeed, in my own case, my only involvement personally has been in the review of the Milly Dowler case, as well as my involvement in Operation Anagram. The latter case involved the nationally-led investigation looking at potential further victims of the convicted killer Peter Tobin, to which I will return shortly. Therefore, in this respect, the Milly Dowler case was unusual.

Amanda Dowler, better known as Milly, was 13 when she went missing during the afternoon of 21st March 2002. She had spent the day at Heathside School, in Weybridge, before

REAL MURDER INVESTIGATIONS

Milly Dowler

catching the train home. Ordinarily she would have left the train at Hersham but had decided to get off one station earlier at Walton to eat in the station café with a friend. Milly phoned her father at 3.47pm, telling him she would be half an hour late getting home. The girls left the café at 4.05pm, with Milly walking home on her own. She was last seen by a friend of her sister, some three minutes later, walking along Station Avenue. A CCTV camera further along the road did not show Milly. So it was clear she had disappeared sometime and somewhere between the sighting by Milly's sister's friend and the CCTV camera. Milly did not return home and was reported missing by her parents at 7pm that evening.

An investigation, known as Operation Ruby, began, initially run by DCI Stuart Gibson, the local crime manager based at Staines Police Station which covered the area. Stuart Gibson had only recently come to Surrey Police on promotion from his previous force, Hertfordshire. It would be correct to say that he had limited experience of murder investigation at any level. It was also the case that Surrey's set up in terms of major crime investigation was limited at this time. Whilst they had teams of officers allocated to such investigations, the highest rank was detective inspector. There were no dedicated SIOs at either DCI or detective superintendent level. This meant that a senior detective, usually from the local area, was nominated as the SIO. This was the case with Stuart Gibson. Such appointments therefore took no account of the level of experience or training of individuals, which was very unfortunate, to say the least.

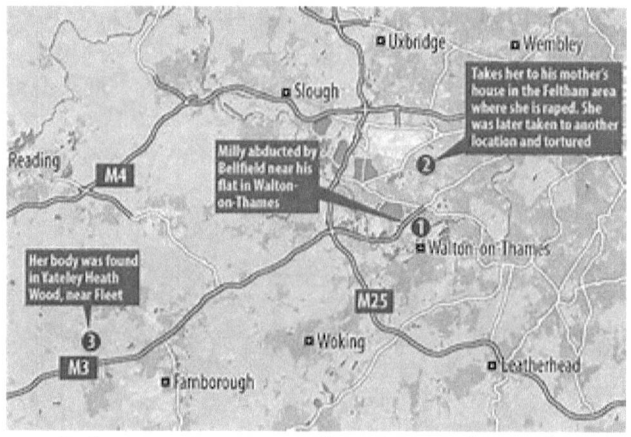

Relevant sites regarding Operation Ruby

Surrey is a medium-sized provincial force. At that time, they averaged around three murders per annum. The vast majority of these fitted into the lower categories, as described earlier. Therefore, it was very rare for them to be tested in the way Sussex Police had been, a couple of years earlier, with the case of the murder of Sarah Payne. Therefore, faced with a case of the magnitude of one involving the disappearance and murder of Milly Dowler, they were not in the best of places. This is not meant as a criticism of those working in Surrey at the time, but rather a statement of fact, recognising the difficulties that this presented to those involved.

REAL MURDER INVESTIGATIONS

During early May 2002, Sussex Police were approached to conduct a review of the investigation. The approach was made by the then Chief Constable Dennis O'Connor to the Sussex Chief, Ken Jones. Sussex were asked due to their experience of the Sarah Payne case, as well as the force's close geographical proximity to Surrey. Jeremy Paine was then Head of Sussex CID and appointed a DCI, John Levett, and some other colleagues representing the various disciplines involved in such investigations, to undertake the review. John had recently returned from sick leave and was therefore available. At the time, I was still operating as an SIO within Sussex. John was a highly competent investigator and very capable of conducting such a review.

Terms of reference for the review were drawn up, agreed and signed off by the respective chief officers. The review quickly identified some key issues. The investigation was suffering from a lack of direction, as well as an apparent excessive focus on Milly's father, Bob Dowler, as the potential offender. Due to the type and nature of the investigation, it had quickly escalated into a massive enquiry and in hindsight, should have focused more on the short period of time when it was ascertained very early on that Milly went missing.

A report was completed, making recommendations, one of which led to the SIO, Stuart Gibson, being replaced by DCI Brian Marjoram, a far more experienced investigator.

As such reports go, it was fairly critical and highlighted the fact that the investigation had, to some extent, lost its way. At this stage, of course, it should be remembered that Milly's body had not been found. This would not happen until 18th September 2002, almost exactly six months after she went missing. The main areas of criticism were that the case had not been treated as a potential murder early enough and that property and clothing belonging to Milly had not been subjected to forensic examination. These were items from her home which, at that stage of the investigation, could have proved important, particularly given the focus on Milly's father. Also, there had been an unnecessary delay in examining Milly's computer.

After the submission of this report, it was agreed that Sussex would continue to support the investigation through a running review, providing the new SIO, Brian Marjoram, with regular weekly updates on any findings. This was the position when I started my new role on promotion to detective superintendent for Homicide Reviews. Having discussed events with John and Jeremy Paine, we all agreed we needed to draw the review to a conclusion. It could not be allowed to be open-ended. As a result, we ensured that all the different elements making up the review were concluded at agreed points and I asked each team leader to supply me with details of their findings and recommendations. I would then draft the final report.

By the time the report was written, Milly's body had been found by mushroom pickers in Yateley Heath Woods, near Yateley in Hampshire. Her badly decomposed body could only be identified through dental records, which meant the cause of death could not be ascertained. There was none of Milly's clothing or possessions present.

The investigation cost a total of £6 million and was, without doubt, the largest investigation ever undertaken by Surrey Police. A total of 3,500 house to house enquiries were conducted, 350 sites searched, and 5,600 statements taken. Fifty registered sex offenders, living within a five-mile radius of Walton on Thames, were traced, interviewed and eliminated from the investigation.

The report that I prepared was extremely detailed, with around 90 recommendations. Out of these, around 50 related to the investigation itself and 40 were linked to suggestions involving changes to be made within the force in terms of its approach to murder investigation. It was

REAL MURDER INVESTIGATIONS

when the report was presented that I learnt a valuable lesson. The report had initially gone to Surrey to have it checked for fact and emphasis. This had taken place but then Jeremy Paine and I were asked to attend a meeting in Surrey with the Deputy Chief Constable, then Bob Quick, in December 2002. When we arrived, there was a room full of people, all representing the different investigative disciplines within the murder investigation. They wished to go through the report recommendation by recommendation, outlining what they intended to do as regards each and every one. Seeing that this could potentially go on not only for that day but also others, I discussed this with Jeremy. It was of no concern to us as to what they were going to do about the report or its recommendations. We had completed the task requested of us. The report was theirs to deal with as they saw fit. Having explained this on our return, we were pleased to be able to withdraw. If recommendations regarding the investigation itself are not going to be progressed, then this is a matter for the SIO to record in their policy book, together with the rationale for not doing so. This would at least provide an answer in the event of any later criticism. Similarly, if recommendations about suggested organisational change are not accepted, then again it would be appropriate to record the rationale as to why not, in answer to any potential later criticism.

There are two elements to the Milly Dowler investigation which are of particular interest. Firstly, in relation to the investigation itself, a red Daewoo Nexia was present on CCTV coverage from the camera previously referred to. This vehicle belonged to Emma Mills, the then girlfriend of Levi Bellfield. This was timed at 4.32pm on the afternoon that Milly went missing. During an interview with Bellfield by police in 2009, he stated that he was driving the vehicle at the time. Also, in terms of the house to house enquiries,

Kevin Moore

Levi Bellfield

whilst the records show 3,500 households were visited, the house in which Levi Bellfield was living with his girlfriend was attended on 11 occasions, without a response being gained. The house was 55 seconds away from the bus stop where Milly was last seen. I have always been of the opinion as an SIO that house to house enquiries are an undervalued element of any investigation. On occasions, it often seems as if some investigators see the process as a box to be ticked, rather than as being of potential benefit. Also, house to house is not always just about who may or may not have seen something relevant. It can be more about a potential suspect(s) living in close proximity to where the incident took place, in this case, Bellfield. Therefore, an unanswered address should never be left as such, however much effort is taken. Clearly, as it was known Milly had walked from the nearby railway station, the relevance of house to house was further enhanced. In this particular case, perhaps the parameters of the house to house may have been too wide i.e. 3,500. It is often better to keep such things focused as regards an achievable target and then this can be completed thoroughly without unnecessary pressure to complete the task. It was known that Milly disappeared before the CCTV

REAL MURDER INVESTIGATIONS

camera, so house to house enquiries could have been kept to fairly tight parameters. As is often the case, hindsight is a wonderful thing! Whilst Bellfield's presence nearby may not necessarily have brought about suspicion, a background check of his criminal history might well have done. This would have happened if he had been seen during the house to house enquiries. Also, if his name had been 'in the system' when Colin Sutton, the SIO from the London cases referred to earlier, approached Surrey Police, a quick check of HOLMES would have revealed his presence at an address very close to where Milly went missing. I think it might be stretching the point to suggest that other crimes of Bellfield's may have been prevented, if he had been seen during the house to house enquiries. To place too great an emphasis on his living at a nearby address, even when put together with him driving the Daewoo nearby, may not have led to him being categorised as a suspect. However, he may have been a 'person of interest'.

Additionally, as regards the investigation itself, another incident could and should have been linked to the case. On the day before Milly disappeared, Rachel Cowles, aged 11, was offered a lift in a red car in Shepperton, Surrey. Her mother reported the incident in a 999 call to police. Neither the call handler or the member of staff who handled the information appreciated the significance of this, when Milly was reported missing subsequently, and it was never passed to Operation Ruby. However, little could be done about this as it is about individuals and, whilst it may have been of interest in general terms to the Dowler investigation, its significance in terms of the red vehicle would not have been appreciated at that stage. However, again, it would have been in the HOLMES system.

The other element related to the Milly Dowler case was, of course, the matter of the phone hacking investigation. A few years ago, I was put on notice that I may be required to appear before the Home Affairs Select Committee in connection with their investigation into phone hacking. However, once they appreciated that the review I had conducted was geared solely to look at the murder investigation rather than side issues, I was not ultimately called.

However, an Independent Police Complaints Commission (IPCC) enquiry in 2013 into the issue, as it related to intrusions into the Dowler family, was highly critical of Surrey Police generally and also some specific officers. Their report stated that Surrey was solely focused on trying to find Milly, who was still missing at that time. This in itself is not an issue, of course. However, the phone hacking matter could and indeed should have been picked up as a separate investigation.

Surrey officers had had a meeting with two *News of the World* reporters in 2002, when discussions had taken place regarding voice messages on Milly's phone. These messages would ultimately be discovered to have been removed, although it was never identified by whom.

Despite now being aware that Milly's phone had been hacked by the *News of the World*, Surrey Police failed to take any action for nearly ten years. The report criticised the fact that even by 2007, the Force were still silent when the official investigations involving the broader phone hacking issue by journalists led to the jailing of a *News of the World* reporter and a private detective, regarding admissions they had made relating to hacking the phones of Royal Household members. The IPCC report pointed out that if Surrey Police had prompted a criminal investigation, even at a later stage, then this may have curtailed this activity more generally at a much earlier stage.

Despite their investigation, the IPCC were unable to identify evidence of who made the decisions not to investigate the matter or indeed why. Reference was made

REAL MURDER INVESTIGATIONS

to an inbuilt fear of the media. Officers told the IPCC that the hacking matter was not investigated in order to keep the media 'onside'. Reference was also made to the media being 'untouchable and all powerful'.

They was also highly critical of senior officers who were described in the report as 'afflicted by a form of collective amnesia' regarding the force's failure to investigate the matter and also to recall who took decisions regarding it. There was considerable criticism of the then Deputy Chief Constable of Surrey Police who was ultimately in charge of the Milly Dowler murder investigation. This criticism, it has to be said, came in the main from other police sources, rather than the IPCC, who seemed to fudge the issue of overall knowledge and responsibility as regards the decision-making of the then DCC. Indeed, some were quite incredulous, it has to be said. The individual concerned received 'Words of Advice', the lowest outcome in terms of sanction. Separately, a Detective Superintendent in Surrey Police also received similar 'Words of Advice'.

The report concluded that many chances had been missed to raise the alarm about phone hacking. The issue of Milly's missing voicemails was also never satisfactorily explained or covered in the report. Therefore, suspicion as regards this still prevails.

My experience of being involved in the Milly Dowler review was of huge benefit in later years. It demonstrated the importance of such processes being conducted with neutrality and integrity. There is absolutely no point in carrying out such reviews unless this is the case.

Earlier, I mentioned I would return to the case of Peter Tobin. It seems appropriate to mention this here, having dealt with the case of Levi Bellfield. Occurrences of serial murder are fortunately fairly rare. When dealing earlier in this book with the case of Jessie Earl, I mentioned the suggestion made by Mark Williams-Thomas of the

Kevin Moore

involvement of Peter Tobin in the deaths of other young women, which included the suggestion of him being involved in the murder of Jessie as well as the disappearance of another young woman from Sussex, Louise Kay.

Following Tobin's conviction for the murder of Angelika Kluk, a 23 year old Polish student, Operation Anagram was set up as a national investigation, looking into the life and movements of Tobin, due to his potential involvement in other murders. This was led by officers in Scotland where the murder of Kluk had taken place. This ultimately led to the recovery of the bodies of Vicky Hamilton, who went missing in February 1991 and Dinah McNicol, who went missing during the same period, with both of them having been buried in the garden of a house in Margate, Kent, previously occupied by Tobin. He was subsequently convicted of both their murders.

Operation Anagram, which began in 2006, ran for some time and, although this led to a further nine cases of missing and murdered females being potentially linked to Tobin, there was no evidence available to charge him with any further offences.

During Operation Anagram, it became clear that Tobin had previous links to Sussex. During my time as Head of Sussex CID, Sussex Police were called upon to make enquiries at a number of addresses that Tobin previously had access to. In 1969, he was 22 years old when he married Margaret Mountney and they lived in a flat two doors away from an eight-bedroom house in Dyke Road, Brighton which had a patioed garden. He also had links to the following addresses in Brighton and Hove: a flat in Grand Parade, Brighton; premises in Eastern Street, Brighton; a flat in Station Road in Portslade, Hove, and a flat in Chadborn Close, Bristol Estate, Brighton. In 1973, he married a nurse named Sylvia Jefferies at St John the Baptist Chapel in Bristol Road, Brighton.

REAL MURDER INVESTIGATIONS

There was no evidence to link Tobin in any way to the death of Jessie Earl and indeed, it did not fit Tobin's usual method of operating, whereby he buried his victims. The other missing young woman from Sussex mentioned was Louise Kay who came from Polegate and went missing in 1988. This was also linked to Tobin by Williams-Thomas in the same TV programme. However, to this day, the body of Louise Kay has never been found and it is speculation that Tobin had any involvement.

Operation Anagram was wound down in June 2011 with no further charges resulting in relation to Peter Tobin.

The cases of Bellfield and Tobin represent my only link to cases involving serial killers and this, it has to be said, was fairly remote involvement, which supports the view that such cases are extremely rare. To emphasise this further, during all of my police service, Sussex Police never investigated, in any direct sense, one instance involving a serial killer.

CHAPTER 9
Unresolved or 'Cold'/Unsolved Cases

Cold or unresolved cases have awoken the imagination of the public, mainly due to fictional portrayals of such investigations. *CSI – Crime Scene Investigation* in the United States, *Waking the Dead,* starring Trevor Eve as Detective Superintendent Peter Boyd, *Silent Witness* and *New Tricks,* with Amanda Redman and Dennis Waterman, have all served to have viewers glued to their televisions.

Of course, in terms of reality, there are many, many such cases which have been variously tabled on such sites as Wikipedia, some even going back centuries. Some of the most notorious are those involving the murders of: Carl Bridgewater, a young boy who was shot dead in September 1978; Suzy Lamplugh, who disappeared on 28th July 1986; and Jill Dando who was shot dead on 26th April 1999. In terms of Sussex, a number have already been the subject of coverage within this book. These include the stabbing to death of schoolboy Keith Lyon on the outskirts of Brighton in 1967, and Margaret Frame strangled and stabbed in October 1978 in Brighton. The list of those relating to Sussex are included below for interest, with some being described in more detail.

In particular, it is developments in forensic science which are mainly focused upon, which is very appropriate as this is likely to provide the single, most realistic prospect of securing belated convictions. I have already demonstrated this in a practical sense in regard to the *Babes in the Wood* murders and the resultant conviction of Russell Bishop. The other potential line of enquiry likely to bear fruit involves witnesses or criminal associates changing their loyalties and giving evidence against those involved. Indeed, under what

REAL MURDER INVESTIGATIONS

is still relatively recent legislation, those either awaiting trial or those serving a sentence, can, dependent upon individual circumstances and with the agreement of the CPS, have their sentences reduced in return for giving evidence. Judges can allow these reductions, based on the value of the evidence given. There have, however, been very few successful outcomes from this source.

One case I recall in Sussex involving a change of loyalty led to the conviction of the man responsible for killing a mother and her 14-year-old daughter at their home in Beach Road, Eastbourne. In the early hours of 6th September 2003, a fire led to the discovery of the bodies of Sally-Anne Baxter-Smith and her daughter, Lois. Two other people present in the building managed to escape. An investigation revealed it was a clear case of arson. In the early stages of the police enquiry, a man named Antony Scrase, aged 35, was arrested, on the basis that his partner, Anna Fitzgerald, had an ex-husband who was apparently attempting to form a relationship with an uninterested Sally-Anne. Scrase was believed to have intervened in the belief that this was what his partner wanted and therefore he became a suspect for the double murder. As there was insufficient evidence at the time to charge him, the investigation eventually went 'cold'. Subsequently, Scrase was arrested, convicted and sentenced to a term of imprisonment for separate and unrelated offences. He had a vast criminal record with 75 previous convictions at the time.

In 2007, after discussions with me as Head of CID, DCI Trevor Bowles, who worked on the Major Crime Branch as an SIO, reopened the case, as Scrase's partner had intimated she would be prepared to assist police by obtaining an admission from Scrase during a prison visit. Scrase had previously confessed to her that he was responsible for the double murder. In other words, her loyalties had changed. This arrangement duly took place and Scrase's admissions, made to her during a visit, were recorded. This was only done after the police had obtained the relevant authorities available under RIPA (The Regulation of Investigatory Powers Act 2000) which governs police use of various surveillance techniques, including technical surveillance as was used here. Scrase was subsequently arrested and charged with the offences. On 9th July 2010, he pleaded guilty and in September 2010, was sentenced to life imprisonment with a minimum tariff of 20 years imprisonment.

So, what is a 'Cold Case'? It can be defined quite simply as normally involving a violent crime, such as murder or rape, that happened some time previously and which police investigators had thoroughly investigated but had been unable to solve. The case therefore becomes 'cold' because of the passage of time. This title within the police was dispensed with, at least in terms of external communications, because of the suggestion that the term may have seemed heartless. Therefore, such cases are more likely to be referred to as unresolved or unsolved. There is an important distinction between undetected/unsolved and unresolved cases. As regards the former, these tend to involve those matters where no real suspect has been identified or there is insufficient evidence to proceed with a prosecution. In relation to the latter, these cases involve those where a conviction has subsequently been overturned and no new suspects are identified. A good example involves the murder of Billie-Jo Jenkins.

There was an expectation that such cases were the subject of regular review. However, this was not the case initially. Therefore, whilst a case may be 'cold', such matters always remain 'open', even if, at a given point in time, all viable investigative leads have been exhausted. Therefore, it can legitimately be said that, whilst some cases might go cold, they never die.

REAL MURDER INVESTIGATIONS

In recent years in the UK, there have been allegations made against a number of celebrities or other high-profile individuals. These mainly involved historic sexual offences, and the conviction of offenders for long term unsolved crimes continues to provide positive publicity. One of these involved the belated conviction in January 2012 of David Norris and Gary Dobson for the murder of Stephen Lawrence, committed in April 1993.

The dilemma for the police is to consider how much effort should be put into solving what are sometimes very historic cases. One practical element involves those cases where it needs to be decided if it is possible for suspects or key witnesses to still be alive. However, it cannot be over-stated how important it is for a victim or their family to achieve some form of closure resulting from a positive outcome. I have already outlined the case of Jessie Earl which highlights this need by the family perfectly. Also, regardless of the rights and wrongs, consideration must be given to the cost and the ability to resource such cases, especially in times of reducing budgets. Most forces have difficulty in maintaining the necessary staffing for current long-running murder investigations, without having to consider this additional burden. The knack therefore is to have in place a process whereby an effective, regular review of such cases can be undertaken without too much wasted time or money.

Looking at such cases has really only taken off since the beginning of the millennium. The first stage was to gather together all the previous case paperwork and exhibits. This, in some cases, was a feat in itself. It needs to be borne in mind that much of this was in paper form and pre-existed HOLMES by many years in some cases. Some key exhibits had not been stored as well as they would be now and therefore there was a potential deterioration in their quality. Some were located in damp basements or garages and in some cases, paperwork or exhibits had even been lost or disposed of. Therefore, getting to a stage where sensible reviews of cases could take place was extremely difficult and often protracted. This task was either given to a capable officer who was on light duties or to a former retired police officer who came back as a police staff member on a contract. A similar situation arose with even the detected murder cases. These too were often stored in an ad-hoc fashion, necessitating a lot of work to pull things together and complete a closing report.

Certainly, in Sussex, all of the above was very much the case at the time of the new millennium. As the reader will recall from the previous chapter regarding reviews, this was something which had to be done, in order to comply with national guidance. We complied with the necessary requirements as best we could, taking into account the passage of time since some cases were closed down. I recall an officer called Heidi West, working in the Hastings area, who did a first-class job in this regard. Now all these cases are centrally filed. When I set up the Major Crime Review Branch for Sussex Police, I was given a budget to recruit some part-time retired police officers who initiated much of what subsequently developed in terms of our unsolved cases. This gave us a real impetus to be able to move things on. Whilst not every case looked at led to the identification of new lines of enquiry, at the very least we were able to get ourselves to a point where cases could be picked up by somebody at a later date, who would know by reading the current situation report what the position was.

The moral element of such cases cannot be ignored. The first conference I attended as a member of the International Homicide Investigators Association in Las Vegas in 2003 was entitled *Never Forgotten* and its focus was on cold or unsolved cases. There was a huge amount of learning to be done during the course of the conference, which we were able to take back to the UK, and Sussex specifically.

REAL MURDER INVESTIGATIONS

'Cold' case successes, however achieved, can inspire public confidence in that a successful outcome demonstrates a commitment to obtaining justice for a victim and/or their family. No one wants to witness dangerous offenders getting away with crimes of violence. Therefore, the moral aspect cannot be overstated. This was best evidenced in the case of Stephen Lawrence. There is no doubt whatsoever that Stephen's family were let down by the police and when this became public knowledge, served to undermine confidence in the Metropolitan Police and policing more generally. However, with the cuts to police budgets, there are inevitably risks that such matters will not always receive the prioritisation that they deserve.

My case study to demonstrate the value of dealing with unsolved and unresolved investigations involves the murder of Julian Webb by a woman known at the time of her conviction as Dena Thompson. As is often the case when a woman is guilty of murdering a spouse or partner, the media referred to her as the 'Black Widow'.

The irony of the conviction, which was achieved in December 2003, was that the case involving the death of Julian Webb, who had died in 1994, was re-opened in 2002 after Dena Thompson was found not guilty of the attempted murder of her husband Richard, whom she had married in 1998. During that trial held at Lewes Crown Court in 2001, she admitted to 15 counts of deception involving securing money from three former lovers, including Thompson, and she was jailed for three years and nine months. The attempted murder charge itself related to the fact that Richard Thompson had been bound and gagged as part of some perverted sex game. Dena Thompson beat him with a baseball bat and also cut him with a knife, causing serious injuries from which he later recovered. During the trial, she had claimed she had acted in self-defence as a result of her husband attacking her, after he discovered that she had defrauded him.

The case involving the death of Julian Webb had not, at the time it occurred, even been categorised as murder. It had been made the subject of an investigation but having not been in a position to secure sufficient evidence against Dena Webb, as she was then, the case had been concluded at that point.

Julian Webb and Dena Thompson

The fact that ultimately Dena Thompson was convicted of Julian's murder was due, in no small part, to his mother's persistence. Rosemary Webb, a retired teacher from Hayling Island, was adamant her son had neither committed suicide nor suddenly been taken ill. She was suspicious of Dena Thompson from the start of her son's whirlwind romance over a three-month period in 1991, leading to the pair marrying. It transpired that the marriage was bigamous as Thompson was still married to a man named Lee Wyatt.

At the time of her son's death, Rosemary's shock and grief quickly turned to anger when she found out that Dena had

REAL MURDER INVESTIGATIONS

turned up at her son's work place, the Portsmouth News Group, asking for his £36,000 death benefit. As a result, Mrs Webb had set about proving she was legally the next of kin, having discovered that Dena was still married to Lee Wyatt, with whom she had a son, Darren.

Julian died in June 1994 on his 31st birthday, at the home he shared with Dena in Yapton, West Sussex, after he had eaten a 'hot' curry. The case was re-opened when a witness made reference to this and a belief developed that Julian, who had died as a result of consuming an excessive amount of prescription (anti-depressants) and non-prescription drugs (aspirin), had been the victim of murder. The view was that the drugs had been hidden in the curry. Whilst this was pursued as a potential explanation during the original investigation following Julian's death, there was insufficient evidence to show that Dena was responsible. In addition, that investigation did not have the advantage of being in possession of the evidence and information which arose subsequent to Julian's death. Rosemary Webb was of the view that her son, who had spoken to her, sometime before his death, of a planned fishing trip and a move to Florida, would not have contemplated suicide as there was no reason for this. She had spoken to Dena on the day of Julian's 31st birthday, only to be told he was too ill to speak to her or to open his cards or presents. It was that night that Dena Thompson called an ambulance, but Julian was found to be dead, and it was believed he had died hours previously. Rosemary was suspicious of the lack of concern shown by Dena. The post mortem confirmed the death as being caused by the overdose and subsequently an open verdict was recorded by the Coroner.

I was asked to oversee the investigation run by DCI Martyn Underhill who had been involved previously with the Richard Thompson investigation. It was an unusual case as, in the initial stages, we obtained permission to exhume

Kevin Moore

Julian's body. This was my one and only experience of such matters. The fact that we were able to do this was due to Julian's mother insisting, against Dena's wishes, to have Julian buried, rather than cremated. She was also very happy to give her consent to the exhumation which undoubtedly speeded up the whole process.

It was discovered that, during her marriage to Julian, she had stolen £23,000 from the Woolwich Building Society where she worked and she had subsequently been jailed for this offence in 1995. Legal reasons prevented this, and matters involving her other previous convictions, being mentioned at her later trial for the murder of Julian Webb.

During the investigation, we had the distinct advantage of having in our possession all the matters that had occurred following the death of Julian Webb. It is clear that Dena Thompson was involved over many years in developing numerous stories which convinced several men to agree to certain courses of action which operated to her benefit. Underpinning this was a determination on her part to establish the financial status of each of her male partners/husbands. She then used a concoction of various lies in order to relieve them of their money. This even included telling people she was dying from cancer and convincing both Julian and subsequently, Richard Thompson, to move to Florida.

During her trial at the Old Bailey in November and December 2003, we were extremely well served by Michael Birnbaum QC. He had been meticulous in planning how he would present the prosecution case and ensured that we furnished him with the evidence necessary for him to achieve this. The case very much revolved around the fact that, at the time of his death, Julian Webb had been neither suicidal nor ill. He had told many friends and colleagues of both short and longer term plans. Therefore, it was highly unlikely he would have taken his own life. Similarly, there was nothing to suggest he had been suffering from any illness. If this was accepted, it then became a case of who was responsible for administering the fatal dosages of drugs? Coupled with the fact that Dena could seemingly have been the only person likely to have done this, there was also the issue involving the timing of her calling the ambulance. It was apparent that Julian had been dead for some time before she made the call. Then there was her obsession with obtaining the death benefit so soon after Julian's death, and the fact that she was determined to have Julian cremated. Once all the circumstances were pieced together, a clear picture began to emerge.

On Friday 12th December 2003, the jury found Thompson guilty of Julian's murder. She was given a life sentence, with an order that she should serve a minimum of 16 years. Of course, only Thompson truly knows why she killed Julian. However, I believe the facts spoke for themselves. As well as the false claims she made in court against Richard Thompson during her previous trial, she had also made a false claim against former husband Lee Wyatt, involving a serious sexual and physical assault on 8th February 1993. Fortunately for him, Mr Wyatt was able to provide an alibi, which showed him to have been hundreds of miles away at the time. The injuries she had suffered were believed to have been self-inflicted. In closing the case following her sentencing, Michael Hyam QC, the Recorder for London, said, 'What you did was utterly ruthless and without pity. Nothing can excuse you for the wickedness of what you did.'

Rosemary Webb, Julian's mother, attended every day of the month-long trial and gave evidence against Thompson. Thankfully, she saw justice finally achieved for her son.

Subsequently, together with others, I took part in two TV documentaries relating to this case, as inevitably, cases involving women killers do seem to attract considerable media attention.

Kevin Moore

Overall, the case demonstrates to me the value and the moral duty to never allow such matters to be closed permanently. There does need to be a logical approach to reopening so called 'cold' cases. However, if the new or additional evidence is sufficiently compelling, then the outcomes make it all the more worthwhile for all those with an interest.

Unsolved Murders in Sussex

Included below are details of unsolved murders in Sussex. It should be noted that I have not included here the murders of Jessie Earl, Keith Lyon and Margaret Frame, as these have been covered elsewhere in the book. It also needs to be recognised that these are unsolved as opposed to unresolved, remembering the definitions previously given.

Gordon Orville Donovan 1st January 2004

Gordon Donovan was found dead inside a plastic barrel beneath cliffs at Beachy Head near Eastbourne. He had been bound and gagged, had his face slashed, and was found to have been stabbed in the back with a screwdriver. An inquest into his death revealed he died from a stab wound in the back that had ruptured his kidney.

Police investigators spent six weeks attempting to identify him but were only able to confirm his identity after an unrelated Met investigation into a robbery at a café in Brixton uncovered a 'heavily bloodstained chair'. DNA forensics later confirmed the blood matched Gordon's records and it is believed he was murdered in the café.

Three men were arrested in 2004 but no one was charged or convicted.

Jennifer Kiely 22nd January 2005

Jennifer Kiely was 35 when she was found dead in a seafront shelter at the Holywell end of Eastbourne. An investigation

REAL MURDER INVESTIGATIONS

revealed she had been sexually assaulted, stabbed, and set on fire. A detective is reported to have commented: 'I can say from her injuries that this attack was sustained with a high degree of ferocity.'

Police viewed more than 1,800 hours of CCTV footage in a bid to find her killer, leading to the arrest of two suspects. However, not enough evidence was found to make any charges and the suspects were released.

Marek Pudlowski 3rd August 2009
Mr Pudlowski was found dead, lying on a bench in Bognor Regis town centre. An examination revealed he had been assaulted extensively in the moments leading up to his death.

William Howe 9th January 1990
Retired 63-year-old vet, William Howe, was found murdered and lying face down in his flat in Victoria Road, Worthing, having been brutally tortured. His legs and arms had been bound with electrical tape, he had been attacked with a hammer and possibly fists, with his attacker having also stamped or kneeled on the small of his back, fracturing his ribs.

An investigation suggested that the attacker may have been looking for a safe, containing tens of thousands of pounds, concealed in the ransacked flat, which was not found by the murderer.

Gary Collins 3rd March 1983
The 25-year-old drugs dealer was discovered stabbed and beaten to death in woods at Brightling, near Battle. Collins had a fractured skull, five stab wounds in the back and his throat had been cut. Detectives believe it may have been a contract killing. He had disappeared from his home in St Thomas Road, Hastings, three months before his body was found. Beside him was the body of his much-loved cross-

Kevin Moore

bred collie, Trudy, who had been stabbed through the heart. Collins' grey BMW car was found abandoned at Battle rail station and police think he may have been forced from the vehicle or led into the woods on the pretext of a drugs deal.

Police inquiries were carried out in London, where many of his drugs deals were made, and in virtually every county in the country, but to no avail. Checks were also made in Sweden, Italy and Belgium, but vital clues remained elusive. At one point, Sussex Police asked the FBI to question several people from Kent who were in custody in America on drugs charges.

Vishal Mehrotra 1981

The skull and several rib bones of this eight-year-old boy were discovered in 1982 by pigeon shooters in remote marshland at Durford Abbey Farm, Rogate, near Midhurst.

Vishal vanished from his home in Putney, south-west London, while shopping with his nanny and sister, seven months earlier, shortly after watching TV coverage of the wedding of Lady Diana and Prince Charles. Police in London launched a massive hunt for the Indian boy, searching wasteland and asking residents to check outbuildings and gardens. After hearing of his death, the boy's father broke down in tears.

A mystery letter writer, who told police he might know the identity of a man who had driven to Rogate from Putney on the Royal Wedding day, was later traced but soon afterwards the trail went cold.

Peter Thurgood and Lindy Benstead 22nd April 1986

The shotgun murder of these two lovers stunned the normally peaceful village of Rake, near Midhurst. They were blasted at point-blank range in a lover's lane, just off the A3. Lindy Benstead, 49, a married mother-of-three, and divorced bricklayer Peter Thurgood, 47, lived in adjoining

REAL MURDER INVESTIGATIONS

Hampshire villages, close to the West Sussex border. Their affair was common knowledge locally.

On the day of the murders, Peter hired a silver Mazda and drove to the Old Thorns Golf Club, Liphook, where Lindy worked as a cleaner. They drove to the track north of Midhurst. A few hours later, a salesman who stopped for a rest discovered Peter slumped by the side of the car with gunshot wounds to his head and chest. Police think Lindy made a desperate attempt to escape as the killer reloaded the double-barrelled shotgun. She managed only a few yards before being shot in the head. Her husband was questioned about the killings but was able to establish a clear alibi.

Robert (Bobby) Jones 31st January 1996
A knife was plunged into the neck of this drugs dealer, whose body was discovered on a grassy bank at the edge of Alexandra Park, Hastings. An inquest in August of that year heard how the victim had told friends he was going to the park to meet some friends who would sell him some drugs, the night before his body was found.

In February 1997, four men were arrested, following raids on addresses in Crawley and Hastings, and in West Malling, Kent. Armed officers arrested two of the men at the Kent address. All four were later released without charge and the case remains unsolved. More than 100 mourners packed Hastings Crematorium for the funeral service for Mr Jones, 27, of Rock Lane, Ore.

Richard Watson 10th December 1996
Mr Watson, 55, was gunned down in the garden of the family home in Holtye Road, East Grinstead. The father-of-four was shot in the chest as he left his blue TVR Chimera sports car outside his semi-detached home.

Richard Watson's third wife, Linda, a former Page 3 girl, and her 25-year-old daughter, Amanda London-Williams, were charged with the killing. They were later found not guilty after the Crown Prosecution Service offered no evidence at the Old Bailey.

An inquest was adjourned as police continued their inquiries into a mystery gunman, believed to have carried out the shooting. So far, no one has been identified. At the same hearing Mrs Watson, 43, and then living in Scotland, clashed with police about the way the case was being dealt with and said details should be examined in public.

Valerie Graves 30th December 2013
Valerie Graves' body was found in her bedroom at a house she and other members of her family were housesitting for friends in Smugglers Lane, Bosham, West Sussex. She had suffered severe head and facial injuries. A patio door, leading directly from the bedroom outside to the back of the premises, was found to be unlocked.

A few days after the murder, a hammer was found by police at the entrance to the driveway of Harts' Farm on Hoe Lane, some 600m from the murder scene. The hammer was confirmed as the murder weapon. A local man was arrested on 14th January 2014 and questioned about the murder but was bailed and released without further action.

In November 2014, a partial DNA profile for the suspect was obtained. In January 2015, Sussex Police began a voluntary mass DNA screening programme in Bosham, asking men aged 17 and over to give samples. At the time, officers had interviewed 9,500 people in relation to the case, a reward of £20,000 had been offered and the murder had been featured on *Crimewatch*. A reward of £10,000 for information leading to the arrest of the person(s) responsible for her murder still remains.

In July 2019, as this book was going to press, a man named Cristian Sabon, a Romanian national, was arrested at his home in Dej, Romania, and has been extradited to the

REAL MURDER INVESTIGATIONS

UK where he has been charged with the murder. Obviously, criminal proceedings are now awaited.

Elaine Taggart 14th January 2008
Elaine Taggart, 48, from Ferring Village, West Sussex, was last seen on January 3rd 2008 when she gave a colleague a lift home from work. Her red Fiat Punto was found on 4th January, a short distance from Goring railway station and a five-minute drive from her home.

Her husband was arrested during the course of the investigation on suspicion of her murder. However, neither he nor anyone else has been convicted and her body has never been located. She was declared as presumed dead for the purposes of her estate on 8th January 2015.

Ian Gow 30th July 1990
In the early hours, a bomb was planted under Gow's Austin Montego car, parked in the driveway of his house in Hankham, near Pevensey in East Sussex. The 4½lb Semtex bomb detonated at 8.39am as Gow reversed out of his driveway, leaving him with severe wounds to his lower body. He died ten minutes later. The IRA claimed responsibility, stating he was targeted because he was a 'close personal associate' of Margaret Thatcher and because of his role in developing British policy on Northern Ireland.

Louise and Robert Goble 3rd February 1985
A fire occurred in a house in St Helens Road, Hastings, the home of two young children, Louise and Robert Goble, and their parents. During the course of the fire, the parents escaped the building which was of Victorian origin. However, both children sadly died. The fire was of doubtful origin and the ensuing investigation involved a double murder enquiry. Family members were suspected of being involved in starting the fire and a number of arrests were made, including both parents.

Kevin Moore

Torso in Bolney, West Sussex 11th October 1991

A man, walking home to Burgess Hill from Cuckfield, discovered a torso in woods off Broxmead Lane in Bolney, Sussex. The remains were found to be of a male, believed to have been in his 60s. The head and hands had been removed and were never found One arm had been severed six inches below the elbow and the other two inches below the elbow, which appeared to have been done to remove an identifying tattoo. The arms and head appeared to have been removed with an axe or bolt cropper. The victim was described as white, had a protruding belly, was circumcised and had a small star-shaped mole on his right thigh. The victim was wearing turned up trousers from Fosters and a blue shirt with a distinctive motif on the pocket.

The investigation to find the identity of the victim and the murder was assigned the name Operation A23 and employed 60 people. DCI Peter Kennett led the initial inquiry. Detectives searched files of over 100 missing men without finding a match, and appeals for the public to come forward with an identity were also fruitless.

In December 1991, police were contacted by a local estate agent with a potential lead; a large rented house in Copyhold Lane, Cuckfield, (1.5 miles from the deposition location of the body) had been abandoned which raised their suspicions. Police investigated the property and found a copy of *Penthouse* magazine, containing an article about dismembering bodies, with numbers scrawled on the pages.

Gunter Josef Knieper, from Dresden, Germany, and Kornelia Maria Teusel first rented the property in September 1991, paying £10,000 (6 months' rent) in advance. The couple abandoned the property sometime around 9th October 1991. Knieper, who had been using the pseudonym Dr Matthias Herrman, was being sought in Germany and Ireland on suspicion of business fraud.

REAL MURDER INVESTIGATIONS

In June 1992, Knieper was arrested in Spain. Police interviewed him in Frankfurt and established that the gang intended to start a fraud operation but Knieper denied any involvement in the murder of the victim. In August 1992, police admitted there was no evidence to link Knieper to the murder. In January 1994, police returned to Germany to interview another unnamed male who had visited the property in Copyhold Lane.

On 2nd August 1994, after a brief service, the remains of the victim were laid to rest at Western Road Cemetery, in Haywards Heath. The coffin bore the name 'Unknown Male' Eight people attended the pauper's funeral, paid for by Mid Sussex District Council. The mourners in attendance were representatives of the police, coroner's office and Mid Sussex District Council.

In December 1995, a few days before Christmas, some flowers and a note were left at the victim's grave. The note bore the message: 'For the unknown male, Peter and team, remember our loss.'

In March 2009, police exhumed the body in the hope that advances in forensic techniques would provide additional information. On 12th November 2009, the case appeared on the BBC programme *Crimewatch*.

In 2010, it was reported that, following media appeals on the UK's *Crimewatch* and its German equivalent, numerous suggestions for the victim's identity had been received. However, none bore fruit. Police stated that three missing persons had been discounted as the victim, and their families had been informed of this.

In 2011, it was revealed that evidence gathered in 2010 indicated that the victim had been dressed post mortem and that the clothes did not belong to the victim. The re-investigation examined a femur, rib bone and toenail from the victim. This suggested that the victim was likely to have come from Southern Germany or a surrounding country.

Kevin Moore

Analysis of the toenail suggested that the victim spent the last year of his life in the UK or the French/German border.

Jillian Matthews 9th November 1981
Jillian Matthews was a lone, vulnerable woman suffering from schizophrenia. She was reported missing in September 1981 and her body was found some six weeks in Mouse Lane, Steyning, West Sussex. She had been raped and strangled.

CHAPTER 10
The Future of Murder Investigation

Having covered a percontentsiod from the early beginnings of murder investigation to the current time, what does the future hold for major crime/murder investigation?

During my service, I have witnessed the very good and the not so good when it comes to the processes involved in murder investigation itself. In the early stages, I saw murder investigations being fully resourced by teams of highly dedicated police officers, determined to achieve a positive outcome. However, despite this, it has to be acknowledged that arguably many of those involved were not fully equipped or best placed to undertake the most difficult of such investigations. There was no learning, as such, to be taught. It was very much a case of following the guidance and practice of those who went before or those who were the most experienced at the time. Neither good nor poor practice was identified and learnt from, as has been the case in the most recent times. Forensic science provision was still in its early stages and certainly DNA profiling was very much a thing for the future. The HOLMES system was some way off and we were still very much tied to old fashioned, previously tried and tested manual indexing and filing. As we have already seen, particular specialisms, now considered part and parcel of any investigation team, had not even been considered, let alone put in place. With this, I am referring to search-trained officers, interviewers, FLOs and of course specialist Major Incident Room operatives, as well as many others that I have discussed previously.

We have moved to where we are now and have been, certainly since the beginning of the current millennium, and things are still developing. I am not suggesting that everything is perfect now, as nothing ever is. However, there is little doubt, things are a lot more professional than they were many years ago. This is not to say that individually detectives are any better now than they were then. However, the current officers are able to draw on many things that were simply not available to SIOs and investigation teams in years gone by. This is a fact, not a criticism. I am content to readily acknowledge that, even since my days of being involved, things have continued to progress in a positive sense. Such developments are a fact of life.

Let us not forget, however, that there was a period around the mid to late 1990s when things were not so good or as well advanced. At the time of the Stephen Lawrence murder in London, the Met were cutting numbers within their AMITs (Area Murder Investigation Teams). Whilst this should not excuse some of the poor decision-making linked to that case, it was certainly subsequently identified that the Met had taken their collective eye off the ball when it came to considering how best to deploy their resources. There was an acknowledgment that these types of crime attract the most attention, especially if and when things go wrong! Organisational as well as individual reputations are at stake and families of victims are let down. Therefore, we need to get things right.

I have already discussed the mistakes made regarding the case involving Jay Abatan's death. This was not the only occasion where we were in the limelight for all the wrong reasons. A brief description of the murder of businessman Richard Watson, which took place in 1996, was included towards the end of the previous chapter, and the case remains unresolved to this day. Following him being shot dead with a shotgun in his own garden at his home in East Grinstead, West Sussex, his third wife Linda and her 25-year-old daughter were jointly charged with his murder. However, the CPS were later to discontinue the proceedings

REAL MURDER INVESTIGATIONS

at court, prior to the trial even starting. The case, as with the Abatan one, was made subject of a review conducted by an outside force, this time the Met. The concluding report was highly critical of the manner in which the investigation was conducted. However, it was the case that things went wrong even before the investigation was commenced, due to a decision to delay the approach of the emergency services to the premises as a result of a shotgun having been fired. Now, inevitably, hindsight is a wonderful thing. However, what cannot be disputed is that this delay resulted in potential critical evidence being lost and therefore the investigation was significantly hampered right from the outset. The usual reference by murder investigators to the so called 'Golden Hour' is again relevant here. Sadly, once a potential opportunity is missed, it nearly always stays missed.

It was these cases as much as anything else, which led to Sussex professionalising their approach to such investigations and bringing about the creation of dedicated SIOs, supported by standalone teams of detectives and other staff, to form what was then called in Sussex, the Major Crime Branch (MCB). The influence for this development also owed itself to a national policing drive for every force to have a similar dedicated team. Therefore, perhaps I was ahead of my time when I proposed such a development in my dissertation for my degree, 'Call in the Yard', mentioned previously! The team still exists, albeit it is now a collaborative approach between Sussex and Surrey Police, and it is known as the Major Crime Investigation Team (MCIT).

The point that I have carefully been building up to is this. We are in a period where the police service is facing financial constraints, the like of which have never been witnessed previously. As I write this, at least a fifth of all police officers have been cut between 2010 and 2018. Similarly, police staff or civilian numbers have also been drastically reduced.

Kevin Moore

There continues to be huge pressure on police budgets. As previously mentioned, during the 1990s, the Met foolishly cut their AMITs and this led to a decline in their ability to be able to investigate murders as thoroughly as they would have liked. I have similarly demonstrated what happens if we use an ad hoc approach to such investigations, similar to the one that Sussex had, prior to the creation of the MCB. Sussex were not alone in suffering from the effects of this. Thankfully, since forces have developed themselves in this way, there have been very few *causes celebres* in this regard. Therefore, it is my contention that, should consideration be made to reducing resources involved, this must be resisted at all costs. The temptation to cut corners in times of scarce resources is considerable. However, the dangers emanating from such a move are very clear in the case studies that I have used. Confidence in the police and organisational reputation is at stake.

Speaking of costs, murder investigation is very expensive. Government figures suggest that the overall cost of a murder, including everything and not just the police investigation, averages £1.8 million. The cost to Cambridgeshire Police of the murders of Holly Wells and Jessica Chapman in Soham by the notorious Ian Huntley, was believed to be in the region of £10 million. By way of a local example, I include here some of the costs of the Sussex investigation into the murder of Sarah Payne at Kingston Gorse, Littlehampton. The 910 police officers and 112 police staff involved at various stages cost £2 million in wages alone. The overtime for just the search team officers amounted to £80,000. The costs for the search team, by day 12 of the investigation, came to £250,000. Forensic Science costs totalled £415,689. Vehicle hire and staff refreshments and subsistence cost £430,000. Therefore, murder investigations don't come cheap, especially in cases which involve those of the highest category/classification.

REAL MURDER INVESTIGATIONS

However, if things go wrong, then the financial costs as well as reputational ones are massive. I have already covered the fact that the reinvestigation of the death of Jay Abatan cost £2 million. During the course of the reinvestigation into the murder of Richard Watson in the early 2000s, in a bid to leave no stone unturned, it was decided to dig up the whole garden of the Watson's address, now occupied by new owners. This was in order to locate shotgun pellets and was part of a wider forensic search undertaken by a private consultant. Whilst this approach, if questionable in terms of value added, (and one or two of us did so at the time), its cost was an eye watering £700,000. To make matters worse, nothing of evidential significance was found. I am sure the occupants were pleased to have their garden landscaped at the expense of Sussex Police! The advances in forensic science techniques are also interesting. I have already described the hugely positive outcome as regards the *Babes in the Wood* murders. However, such work is very expensive. I would like to think that, even in the most austere of times, without wasting money and being discerning in terms of what is achievable through the use of forensic advisors, sensible judgements can be made in deciding what is submitted for examination. What it all boils down to is, what price for success in bringing offenders to justice in cases involving murder? Putting things right costs a great deal, both in terms of the reputation of the police service as well as financially. The message should therefore be, 'Act in haste, repent at leisure!'

I have often been asked by friends and family who have never served in the police as to what upset me the most, as regards dealing with murder and its consequences. Just how did I cope with the harrowing circumstances? Fortunately, I can say it has never affected me psychologically. Without a doubt, the most upsetting are those cases where the victim is a child, particularly a baby, or other very young person.

Kevin Moore

This is because they had their whole lives before them, and these have been ended prematurely through a violent and selfish act at the hands of another human being. I have already described at length the cases of the murders of Nicola Fellows and Karen Hadaway, and that of Billie-Jo Jenkins. I have dealt with a number of cases of unexplained baby deaths, as well as some who sadly were clearly the victims of murder or manslaughter. Often such cases are frustrating to an SIO because there are often two suspects i.e. the parents. This may, of course, be the mother of the child and a partner who is not the father. As a result, whilst there is a potential to charge more than one person, if they were present but did not take part in the violence, known as 'joint enterprise', there is often a reluctance for courts to find cases proven in this way. There is a fear of the potential for a miscarriage of justice because of the difficulty of deciding the level of involvement of an individual involved in a 'joint enterprise'.

'Joint enterprise' can be explained as follows.

The law allows for several people to be charged with the same offence, even though they may have played very different roles in the crime. It can apply to all crimes, but recently it has been used as a way to prosecute homicide - especially in cases involving gangs of young men.

Prosecutions for homicides involving two or more defendants must meet the Crown Prosecution Service's definition of joint enterprise.

However, the fact remains that joint enterprise is a vital prosecuting tool, as acknowledged recently by Alison Saunders, the then Director of Public Prosecutions (DPP). In some cases, it's not very clear because of the circumstances of a case exactly who did what, but if it is known that everyone was participating in the crime, then it helps to be able to prosecute them all, and to put those facts before the court.

REAL MURDER INVESTIGATIONS

It is still the case that someone merely present at the scene but taking no active part in the offence will not face prosecution.

One case that certainly springs to mind where joint enterprise may have become an issue, and one that has remained with me, involved the murder of a two-year-old little boy in Hastings. On 28th December 2000, he was found dead in his cot within a flat where he lived with his mother and her boyfriend. He had sadly been dead for some weeks and his body was in an early stage of decomposition. I am pleased to say that we secured a conviction against the mother's partner as a result of the evidence gathered and therefore some justice was achieved. I think what impacted on me most was that this poor little boy had no hope from the moment he was born. He was living in squalid conditions with parents who didn't care, and his death had been discovered in what was a period of general celebration between Christmas and New Year. He had been dead, and his body abandoned, for some weeks.

Then there was the case involving the deaths of a father and his two young sons at Beachy Head, Eastbourne on 25th June 1997, whilst I was the detective inspector for the area. John Chetwynd, aged 43 years, had been involved in a serious domestic dispute with his wife at their home in London, which led to him beating her unconscious with a baseball bat. Believing he had killed her, he drove his two little boys to Beachy Head, the notorious suicide spot, and jumped over with both of them, killing all three. Unsurprisingly, such events inevitably remain with you forever. I remember thinking two things. Firstly, what was the last thing those poor kids thought about, prior to being forced to jump by their father? Secondly, how on earth did the mother of the two manage to deal with the aftermath?

There was also the case in Peacehaven in August 1993 which I referred to fully in my previous book, *My Way*, when a mother, Tracey Evans, suffering from a severe mental illness, drowned her two boys in the bath, Nicholas aged nine, and Lee aged five. Similar to the case involving the Chetwynd family, I always wondered how the father of those two boys coped. He had left the family home earlier that day to return to his army unit, only to have his life turned completely upside down.

The other cases that always left a mark on me were those where, for whatever reason, I/we could not bring about a successful conclusion. I always felt that, regardless of the circumstances, not only was there no closure for the family but similarly there was no closure for those involved in the investigation. This, unfortunately, is very much the lot of the SIO!

In order to demonstrate the impact of any given case upon the SIO, I wish to draw on the case involving the convicted serial killer Christopher Halliwell. The SIO in the case was a man named Steve Fulcher. During his early service with Sussex Police, he worked for me when I was an SIO at the beginning of the millennium. He later transferred to Wiltshire Police where he was promoted to detective superintendent. When a young woman named Siân O'Callaghan, aged 22 years, went missing, he was appointed as the SIO.

My recollection of Steve was that he was a highly motivated police officer, an extremely thorough detective and overall, a decent man. What was to happen to Steve highlights perfectly the perils of being an SIO and the responsibility that goes with it. Sometimes, you have to be prepared to push the boundaries and be lawfully audacious in terms of solving the most serious of crimes. Steve did that and paid with his job.

The circumstances of the case were that, following him taking over the investigation and Siân's body had still not

REAL MURDER INVESTIGATIONS

Christopher Halliwell

been found, suspicion fell upon a local taxi driver, Christopher Halliwell, aged 47. Enquiries had revealed he had picked up Siân in the early hours of a Saturday in March 2011. Due to the suspicion, Halliwell was made the subject of a police surveillance operation. At a given point, he was seen to purchase a large quantity of tablets and it was believed that he may have been contemplating suicide. Therefore, a decision was taken to arrest him. This was carried out, but rather than take the suspect to the police station, Steve instructed his officers to take Halliwell to a location relevant to the route possibly taken at the time that Siân had disappeared. Whilst this was somewhat unconventional, Steve believed that, if the missing woman was still alive, immediate further questioning was imperative in order to save her life. So typical of Steve, he went to the location himself and was then to become involved in what he later described as the most intensive four hours of his life. He was conversing with Halliwell and building a relationship with him, attempting to get him to say where Siân was. This was proving difficult and Steve was on the point of drawing things to a close, when Halliwell told him he had killed Siân. He took them to a location in the

Kevin Moore

area known as the White Horse, Uffingham, the Ridgeway in Oxfordshire. It was at this point that Halliwell indicated he could direct police to another body.

He took the officers to a field where in 2003, some eight years previously, he had buried a 20-year-old sex worker named Becky Godden. What Steve Fulcher would have immediately appreciated was that, by doing things in the way he had, he had in fact operated in breach of what is known as Code C of the Police and Criminal Evidence Act (PACE). This deals with the rights of individuals under arrest, in terms of their detention and questioning. Although Halliwell had been cautioned twice, this should have happened again at the point where Halliwell indicated his involvement in the second murder. Steve should also have reminded Halliwell that he had the right to speak to a solicitor. The irony of this is that, in all probability, Halliwell would have declined as things were moving in line with what he was already saying. A criminal lawyer may well, of course, oppose this, by saying that, if this had been offered to Halliwell, he may not have gone on to incriminate himself. As I have mentioned before, sadly our criminal justice system is not necessarily about a search for the truth but rather compliance with a process! Steve will, of course, argue that he was operating from a moral standpoint and that it was the right thing to do in the circumstances.

Sadly, in 2014, Steve Fulcher was found guilty of gross misconduct, following an IPCC (now IOPC) investigation. His actions were described as 'catastrophic'. In court, Halliwell's barrister attempted to claim that his client's family had been threatened and that Halliwell's confession had been elicited whilst he was under duress. At the time, the evidence obtained regarding the murder of Becky Godden was ruled inadmissible in court.

Although Steve was not dismissed from the service, he had to take sick leave and was suffering from depression.

REAL MURDER INVESTIGATIONS

Quite properly, he received public backing from the families of the two dead woman. In the case of Becky Godden, her mother started a petition, seeking a change in PACE in such circumstances as were faced in this case. Ultimately, Steve chose to resign in 2014, as he felt this was his only option. A truly sad and unnecessary end to his career.

In 2016, a judge, Sir John Griffith Williamson, determined that the evidence gathered in relation to the Becky Godden case could and should be heard in court. Due to this, Halliwell was later found guilty of the murder, and common sense belatedly prevailed. Halliwell, it was determined, will never be released from custody. However, what price has been paid by an individual, trying their best to do their job?

In addition to the damage done to Steve Fulcher's career, it is clear that, potentially at least, Halliwell may well be guilty of other crimes. There is an eight-year gap between the murders of Siân O'Callaghan and Becky Godden. This suggests that he may well be guilty of other offences, as he appears to fit the profile of a serial killer. He may have been inclined to admit further offences, if indeed he is guilty of any, if proceedings at court had been run differently in the first place, rather than the evidence involving the Godden case being dismissed. There is, of course, even at this stage, no reason why the police cannot explore this possibility further. However, with what has taken place, I am guessing it is a classic case of 'once bitten, twice shy'. Sadly, given the circumstances, it is highly unlikely that any senior police officer wants to run the risk of subjecting either themselves or the service to the potential for further criticism. This is even though the course of action pursued was ultimately quite correctly supported through the judicial process.

So, this begs the ultimate question, would I or others have done the same thing, given the exact same circumstances? The issue is a technical one. It is about the

Kevin Moore

need to utter a few key words. I like to think that, in my own case, such an oversight would not occur. However, if it inadvertently did, I would like to think that the justice system would apply some common sense and acknowledge the simple fact that, even allowing for the error, the offender did actually admit the crime and identify where the body was buried! Surely this is the most important thing of all. I would also hope that SIOs and other investigators would receive the full support of police bosses in such circumstances. In some cases, I know that would happen. In others? Well, I am not so sure!

In the context of this final chapter, I have, I hope, in providing the circumstances of the Halliwell case, shown how important it is that we can still recruit the very best SIOs and other investigators to undertake murder investigations. We need to encourage individuals who possess the right calibre, skills and experience to consider putting themselves forward. We need to ensure that we support them in this.

For me personally, and despite what I have just written regarding the experience of Steve Fulcher, I would like to say that I thoroughly enjoyed my time involved in the investigation of murder. Some close to me have commented that I was never happier than when I was called out in the middle of the night, having been presented with circumstances involving a potential murder. As the Homicide Investigator's Creed states, there is truly no greater honour for any individual than to be given the task of investigating the death of another human being. Most of us involved in such cases readily accepted that, when things were going well as an SIO, you were everybody's friend, especially within the organisation. When things were tough, you very quickly learned who your real friends were, and perhaps Steve Fulcher should have expected a lot more support than that which he received.

REAL MURDER INVESTIGATIONS

Of course, as an SIO, or indeed as any investigator involved in murder investigation, we all want to clear up every case with a positive outcome. However, sometimes we just need to grudgingly accept that on occasions, our best may just not be good enough!

BIBLIOGRAPHY

Argus News, Police Reopen Murder Files. 16th February 2000 online

Argus News, Black Widow: Inside the mind of a predator, 16th December 2003 – online

Argus, The mother of an art student who went missing 32 years ago this week says the mystery will one day be solved. 19th May 2012 online

Argus, Detectives have arrested four men after two men were murdered 14 years ago. 25th February 2015 online

Association of Chief Police Officers, *Major Incident Room Standardised Administrative Procedures*

Association of Chief Police Officers, *Murder Investigation Manual*

Athwal, Harmit, Institute of Race Relations. 14th August 2014 online

Barlow, Aidan, Russell Bishop murder trial, Day 4 *Argus* 19th October 2018 online

BBC. *A Week in the Life of a London Murder Detective.* Danny Shaw. 23rd January 2019 online

BBC News, *Murder of Jimmy Millen. Motor cycle key to shooting.* 25th October 2001 online

BBC News, *Police deny Milly inquiry 'blunders'.* 30th June 2002 online

BBC News, *Brighton attack victim Jay Abatan unlawfully killed.* 25th October 2010 online

BBC News, *A man who was acquitted of murdering vicar who he claimed abused him has been found guilty of killing a supermarket worker who he had sex with.* 11th May 2012 online

BBC News, *Four men have been arrested in connection with the murders of two men in Hastings, East Sussex, 14 years ago.* 25th February 2015 online

BBC News, *The parents of an art student who went missing nearly 40 years ago have said the recorded cause of her death should be overturned.* 25th September 2018 online

Bielenberg, Kim, *Our fascination with women who kill: A look at why female killers keep us hooked.* Independent Irish News 7th February 2019 online

Blake, Matt, *A former altar boy vigilante who murdered a gay man he wrongly believed to be a paedophile was told today he may spend the rest of his life behind bars.* Daily Mail 22nd May 2012 online

Bonn, Scott, *Our curious fascination with serial killers.* Psychology Today 23rd October 2017 online

Bonn, Scott, *Why we are drawn to true crime shows.* Times 8th January 2016 online

Bramhall, Andrea, *The Great British fascination with murder.* Ylva Publishing online

Brown, Vanessa, *Why people are obsessed with murder?* news.com.au 16th January 2016 online

Cook, Tony and Tattersall, Andy, *Blackstones Senior Investigating Officers Handbook*

Cowan, Rosie, *'Black Widow' jailed for life for killing husband.* Guardian. 16th December 2003 – online

Curtis, Joseph, *Mother of murdered schoolgirl Billie-Jo Jenkins calls for police to reopen the case on the 20th anniversary of the 13-year-old's death.* Mail online

Dawlish Chronicles. The Victorian fascination with murder. 2017 online

Evans, Sophie and Laws, Peter, *A grisly fascination: Why the British public is gripped by murderers and their horrific crimes.* Mirror News 14th February 2017 online

Evening Standard, Family of murdered Billie-Jo: We're glad Siôn Jenkins was refused compensation. 10th August 2010 online

Furness, Hannah, *Fascination with murder is a product of being civilized.* Telegraph Media 17th September 2013

Guardian, *Teenager convicted of clergyman's murder*. 21st June 2002 online

Guardian. *Police did nothing about Dowler phone hacking for a decade, says IPCC*. Vikram Dodd. 24th April 2013 online

Hastings and St Leonards Observer. *Family Says Jimmy Millen killed Jason*. 21st June 2002 online

Hughes, Mark, *Babes in the Wood Murder: 23 years on, father's first interview*. The Independent 29th June 2009 online

Independent, Adam Lusher. *'Paedophile killer trapped by DNA three decades after murdering two girls,' court hears*. 19th October 2018 online

ITV Meridian News, *Calls for public enquiry after Jay Abatan's death*. 14th August 2014 online

Lewis, Tim, *'How I caught a serial killer – and lost my career in the police'*. The Observer 25th June 2017 online

Lusher, Adam, *Independent* 23rd November 2018 online

Russell Bishop found guilty of 1986 Wild Park murders. Sussex Police News 10th December 2018 online

Mackin, Annette, *Jay Abatan's family asks, 'how close were the police to the men who killed him?' Socialist Worker* 19th August 2014 online

Mattiuzzi, Paul, *Why are we so fascinated with murder? Everyday Psychology* 24th May 2011 online

McEwan, Fergus, *Murder of Jason Martin-Smith. 24th August 2015* Surrey Live online

Mirror. *Billie-Jo Murder Trial: What the jury was not told*. Adrian Shaw. 10th February 2006 online

Moreton, Cole, and Goodchild, Sophie, *Three trials and nine years after the murder of his foster-daughter, Siôn Jenkins is hit by fresh claims about his character*. The Independent 12th February 2006 online

Muller, Robert, *Fascination with Murder – Should you be concerned about it? Psychology Today* 24th May 2018

Olden, Mark. *What happened next?* The Observer 30th May 2004 online

Pidd, Helen, *Man accused of murdering elderly vicar brings new claim of sexual abuse.* 31st August 2010 online

Powell, Laura, Brown, and Mick, Gatenby, Alex, *Art student Jessie Earl disappeared 38 years ago. Has the mystery of her murder finally been solved?* The Telegraph News 21st September 2018 online

Sherlock, Peter, *Jay Abatan's brother's long fight for justice.* BBC News 25th October 2010 online

Sherlock, Peter, *Milly Dowler murder: Surrey Police say mistakes made.* BBC News 24th June 2011 online

Sun, *COLD CASE When did Jessie Earl disappear, was her death linked to serial killer Peter Tobin and what has Mark Williams-Thomas found?* 19th April 2018 online

Sussex Argus. *Revealed: how a gang burglary escalated into a brutal revenge murder.* 22nd August 2015 online

Taylor, Polly, *In the days following the murder of her daughter, Lois started to suspect her husband.* True Crime 17th April 2018 online

Telegraph News, *Suspect in accountant's killing found dead.* 11th June 2003 online

TUC, Justice for Jay Abatan. 9th December 2005 online

Wikipedia, *Babes in the Wood Murders* (Wild Park) online

Wikipedia, Billie-Jo Jenkins online

Wikipedia, Dena Thompson online

Wikipedia, Jane Longhurst online

Wikipedia, Jeremy Bamber online

Wikipedia, Milly Dowler online

Wikipedia, Murder online

INDEX

Abatan, Jay, 117, 119, 123-126, 164, 165, 167, 176, 178, 179
Altman QC, Brian, 63
Babes in the Wood, 47, 56, 129, 144, 167, 178, 179
Bacon, DI Malcolm, 62
Bamber, Jeremy, 91-93, 179
Baxter-Smith, Sally Anne, 145
Bell, Peter, 119, 121
Bellfield, Levi, 23, 53, 131, 137-139
Benstead, Lindy, 156
Bick, Peter, 83-84
Bishop, Russell, 41, 57, 59, 61, 62, 64, 144, 176, 178
Black Widow. *See* Dena Thompson
Bridgewater, Carl, 144
Cheeseman, DCI Martin, 121
Chetwynd, John, 169, 170
Clark, Andre, 94, 96
Cold Case. *See* Unresolved Cases
Collins, Gary, 155, 156
Community Impact Assessments, 20
Coutts, Graham, 27, 97, 98, 99
Crimewatch, 158, 161
Curtis, Graham, 119, 121, 124, 177
Daily Mirror, 76, 177, 178
Dando, Jill, 144
Decision-Making Log, 67
Defences, 24, 26
Delagrange, Amelie, 131
Diminished responsibility, 28, 33
Donovan, Gordon, 154
Dowler, Milly, 23, 97, 129, 131-141, 176, 179
Earl, Jessie, 96, 99, 100, 141, 147, 154, 179
Evans, Tracey, 170, 177
Family Liaison Officer, 20, 52, 59, 105, 106, 110
Fellows, Barrie, 63-64

Fellows, Nicola, 41, 56-57, 168
FLO. *See* Family Liaison Officer
Forensics, 40, 41, 44, 47, 52, 56, 59-64, 73, 76, 80-81, 88-90, 102-103, 129-130, 135, 144, 161, 163, 166-167
Frame, Margaret, 13, 44-45, 144, 154
Fulcher, Steve, 170, 172-174
Glazebrook, Rev Ronald, 35, 68, 78-83, 102
Goble, Louise and Robert, 159
Godden, Becky, 172-173
Gow, Ian, 159
Graves, Valerie, 158
Groves, Jason, 80-82
Hadaway, Karen, 41, 56-57, 168
Halliwell, Christopher, 170-174
Hamilton, Vicky, 142
Hamilton-Deeley, Veronica, 96, 123, 124
Hilton, DC Paul, 110
HOLMES, 20, 41, 42, 49-51, 58, 120, 129, 139, 147, 163
House to House, 20
Howe, William, 155
Hunnisctt, Christopher, 35, 79-84
Huntley, Ian, 55, 166
Insanity, 28
Jenkins, Billie-Jo, 68-78, 146, 168, 177-179
Jenkins, Siôn, 68-77, 177, 178
Jones, Robert, 78, 157
Jones, Sir Ken, 121, 124, 126, 129, 135
Kay, Louise, 142-143
Kiely, Jennifer, 154
Knieper, Gunter Josef, 160-161
Lam, Wei-Yi, 101
Lamplugh, Suzy, 144
Lawrence, Stephen, 94, 97, 126, 147, 149, 164
Legal Definitions, 24
Levett, John, 108, 110, 135
Longhurst, Jane, 27, 96-97, 179
Lyon, Keith, 39-40, 144, 154
Major Incident Room, 20, 41, 43, 49, 50, 163, 176
Manhunt, 131
Marshall, Jim, 39

Martin-Smith, Jason, 111-116, 178
Matthews, Jillian, 162
McDonnell, Marsha, 131
McNichol, Dinah, 142
McNicol, Steve, 113-116
Mehrotra, Vishal, 156
Millen, Jimmy, 107-117, 176, 178
Mitigating Circumstances, 27
Murder Investigation Manual, 44, 66, 127, 176
News of the World, 140
Observer, Hastings & St Leonards, 116, 178, 179
O'Callaghan, Siân, 170-173
Operation Anagram, 23, 132, 142-143
Operation Ruby, 133-134, 139
Paine, Jeremy, 77, 135-137
Payne, Sarah, 134-135, 166
Police Search Adviser, 43, 53
Post-natal depression, 28
Probert, DS Ken, 121
Provocation, 27, 34
Pudlowski, Marek, 155
Reviews, 126, 128, 136
Scenes of Crime, 20
Scrase, Anthony, 145-146
Search teams, 20
Searle, Mark, 113-116
Senior Investigating Officer, 21, 39, 65
Senior Investigating Officers Handbook, 66, 177
Sentencing, 29
SIO. *See* Senior Investigating Officer
Surrey Police, 23, 131, 133, 134, 135, 136, 137, 139, 140, 141, 165, 178, 179
Sutcliffe, Peter, 42
Sutton, DCI Colin, 131, 139
Taggart, Elaine, 159
Tai, Sze-Hau, 101
Taylor, DS John, 91, 179
Thompson, Dena, 149-153, 179
Thurgood, Peter, 156
Tobin, Peter, 23, 100, 132, 141-143, 179

Torpey, Frank, 113-115
Unresolved Cases, 40, 129, 144, 146, 149, 154, 164
Watson, Richard, 126, 157-158, 164, 167
Webb, Julian, 149-152
Webb, Rosemary, 150-151
Wells, DS Bernie, 55, 58
Williams-Thomas, Mark, 100, 141, 143, 179
Yorkshire Ripper, 42

AUTHOR'S BIOGRAPHY

Kevin Moore joined Sussex Police at the age of twenty-one years in June 1978.

After joining, the author spent his two-year probationary period at Brighton during which time he operated as a beat officer and area car driver/observer. Whilst there, he experienced a wide variety of policing situations as one would expect in terms of the cosmopolitan nature of a City the size Brighton and Hove. Following this, he became a rural beat patrol officer at Camber near Rye in East Sussex.

A short while later, he entered the Criminal Investigation Department (CID), as a detective constable. This proved to be the beginning of a long and productive career as a detective during which time he climbed the ranks ultimately achieving the highest rank possible in the CID world of Detective Chief Superintendent when he was the Head of Sussex's CID. During his service he was the senior detective in charge of the CID at Hastings and Eastbourne. He also worked within the Professional Standards Department investigating complaints made against police officers.

He also served as the Chief Superintendent and Divisional Commander of Brighton and Hove during which time he was responsible for all police operations in the City as well as working with key partner agencies including the City's Council. He took command of many large-scale public order demonstrations as well as other major public safety events.

During his detective career, he was a Senior Investigating Officer (SIO) with a responsibility for leading enquiries into homicide and other major crime investigations. He was viewed as being a highly competent senior detective. Many of the case studies used in this book involve investigations in which he played a significant role. He was formerly a member of the International Homicide Investigators Association.

Following his retirement as a police officer in 2009 after more than thirty-one years of service, he took up a position with the newly formed S.E. Regional Organised Crime Unit as a member of police staff. This involved the role of the Regional Intelligence Manager and then subsequently that of the S.E. Regional Prison Intelligence Manager. This Unit has an overall responsibility for investigating the criminal activities of those involved in the commission of the most serious types of crime.

He fully retired from the police service in January of 2018.

This is Kevin's second book, following on from the success of *My Way* which was published in August 2018.

He has been married to Ann for over forty-one years and they have two grown up children and five grandchildren. He holds a BA (Hons) Degree in Public Sector and Police Studies and a Post Graduate Diploma in Police Studies. He is interested in football and cricket and is a season ticket holder with Brighton and Hove Albion F.C. and also now spends his time with his and his wife's Golden Retriever dogs and their four horses.

ABOUT THE PUBLISHERS

Saron Publishers has been in existence since 2005, producing niche magazines. Our first venture into books took place in 2016 when we published *The Meanderings of Bing* by Tim Harnden-Taylor. The third offering from Bing, *The Ruminations of Bing,* was published in July 2019. *Minstrel Magic* by Eleanor Pritchard came out in 2017 and tells the phenomenal show business story of the George Mitchell Singers and the Black and White Minstrels. Further publications planned for 2019 include *Jackie*, the second book in the *Life and Soul* series by Julie Hamill, and *Cargoes*, an exploration of the work of painter Kenneth D Shoesmith and Poet Laureate John Masefield.

Email info@saronpublishers.co.uk to join our mailing list. We promise no spam.

Visit our website saronpublishers.co.uk to keep up to date and to read reviews of what we've been reading and enjoying.

Follow us on Facebook @saronpublishers.

Follow us on Twitter @saronpublishers.

www.ingramcontent.com/pod-product-compliance
Lightning Source LLC
Chambersburg PA
CBHW021104080526
44587CB00010B/371